The *Cult of* Jabez

The *Cult* of **Jabez**

And the Falling Away of the Church in America

Steve Hopkins

THE CULT OF JABEZ
Published by Bethel Press

©2002 by Steve Hopkins
International Standard Book Number
0-9717612-7-2
Cover design by Printworks

Scripture quotations are from:
The Holy Bible, Authorized or King James Version
(The Bible is God's Word and its use in any form
may not be restricted by copyrights or laws made
by mere men without making Him quite angry!)

For information:
Bethel Press
Box 777
Burnet, Texas 78611

Or visit our website @thecultofjabez.com

TABLE OF CONTENTS

Without the sacrifice and undying love given by my wife,
Sandra, our nine children, Ryan, Rebekah, Emily, Micah, Levi,
Bethany, Hannah, Caleb, and Grace,
and the support and encouragement of our friends and church
this message may never have found it's way to paper. Thank
you Burnet Bible Church for your many prayers.
Thank you Chris and Gaylen for being there for Sandra and
me for so many years.
Thank you Don for providing a decade of friendship and the
modern example of a true saint. Thank you Wade and Kathy
for your support over the years (and the $100. truck,
even if it does use more water than gasoline!).
You all helped make this vision a reality.
And thank you, unknown evangelist in Sudan,
for walking into the villages of Africa
on your knees to preach the Good News.
Your example showed me
that what I thought were "needs" were really luxuries.
Your photograph inspired me to go forward when
I was sure that I could not go on.

To all who- like those Christians in the book of Acts-
look at the riches they have been given- and knowing
what Jesus did for them on the Cross, how they could
never repay such a great debt of love, forsake all they have,
and denying themselves, take up their crosses
and follow Him.

PREFACE

Having been hurt and led astray by
false teachings many years ago,
I can sympathize with all those,
who with pure motivations and a
sincere desire to serve the Lord Jesus,
have been misled
by the modern Jabez preachers.

My prayer is that God
will use this book to quicken
the hearts of Christians
all around the world to the
Truth of His Word
in these last days.

Sandra Hopkins

*"Let no man deceive you
by any means:
for that day shall not come,
except there come
a falling away..."*

II Thessalonians 2:3

1
Bless *ME* Lord

In the fictional Christmas movie "It's a wonderful life", an angel gives George Bailey the opportunity of a lifetime… to see what the world would be like if he had never been born.

After experiencing a day in the life of "Pottersville" where his corner of the world has certainly changed for the worse, George comes to his senses. He no longer wishes he had never been born, but prays with all his heart to be returned to Bedford Falls where he lives the rest of his life a different man.

In the next few moments I want to take you on a similar journey… a fictional journey into the heavenlies.

The Bible tells us in Hebrews chapter 12 we are surrounded by a great cloud of witnesses.

Imagine for a moment that you have been given a great gift, a great opportunity. You have been permitted to sit in the grandstands of heaven along with all the saints of old… to see what they see, to hear what they hear.

Flash! There you are, a spectator in the heavenlies surrounded by a great crowd of saints. You look around you and see off to the right the Apostle Paul, who in the book of Acts was hand chosen by Jesus on the road to Damascus. He was jailed, beaten, stoned, shipwrecked, robbed, and eventually beheaded at Rome for his persistent preaching of the Gospel.

Then you notice that just below you is seated a whole row of Jesus' disciples.

There's James, "the Just", who was the leader of the church at Jerusalem, until the Jews threw him head first off the pinnacle of the temple for refusing to deny Jesus before the crowds below. When he survived the fall his enemies beat him to death with a fuller's club.

Next to him you see Mark, a writer of one of the four gospels. Mark was preaching Jesus in Alexandria, Egypt when a mob decided to silence him. He was tied to horses and dragged through the city streets until he died.

And there to his left is Luke, the author of the third Gospel, who laid down his life for the Lord in Greece, being hanged on a tree.

Then down another row or two you see Peter, who was the first of the apostles to recognize Christ as the "Son of the Living God". He was imprisoned on more than one occasion finally suffering martyrdom outside the city of Rome as soldiers crucified him upside down on a cross.

Andrew, John, Phillip, and Stephen, the first Christian martyr are all there around you.

Unable to even catch your breath your attention is drawn to the great attraction below the grandstands.... the heavens seem to roll open like a scroll. And like a giant big screen TV you see the earth below and the events of our time unfolding like a motion picture.

Zoom! The scene appears to be somewhere in the jungles of Africa. It is! It's a village in South Sudan. The camera pans a small group of grass huts.   You see a man riding on a donkey entering the city on a dust choked road.

The sun is bearing down on him, and you realize that he's carrying a Bible in one hand. He is a traveling evangelist, yet not at all like those you've seen and heard on television back home in America. He is obviously very poor, with only one change of clothing and a canteen of water.

As he dismounts you begin to cry. He is lowering himself to the ground by a rope and is walking on his bare knees. He has no feet. A man in the seat next to you explains how Muslim soldiers cut off his feet to keep him from spreading the Gospel. He continues preaching to anyone who will listen.

Zoom! "What is this place," you ask. A woman in the seat above you whispers, "North Korea, shhhh". A group of people are singing hymns in a small one room apartment. Suddenly the door is kicked in. North Korean military police are shouting at the people, pointing their automatic rifles at them. The officer in charge begins to laugh. He takes what appears to be a Bible from one of them and throws it on the floor.

"He's telling them to spit on the Book and they will be set free".

One by one these believers, beginning with their pastor, begin to spit on the Holy Scriptures and run out the door. But then you watch as a young Korean girl kneels down in front of the Bible, tears streaming down her face, as she begins to wipe the spit off the cover with the corner of her dress. The officer in charge aims his weapon at her head and pulls the trigger blowing her brains out all over the floor.

Flash! China. It's Christmas Eve 2000. The Chinese Communists have ordered the destruction of all known unregistered "underground" churches in the Province of Zhejiang. While the Christmas tree lights made by Pastor Li Dexian, and other arrested Chinese believers in slave labor camps, twinkle on American Christmas trees all across our country, the communist People's Liberation Army bulldoze, bomb, and burn over 300 Christian and Catholic churches.

Almost immediately you begin to hear voices rising from the earth. At first the voices are faint.

From Africa you hear the sound of hundreds, like the evangelist who travels by donkey, crying out to God in the night, "Father in heaven, hear our prayer... help us to open our mouths boldly to make known the mystery of the Gospel that many may come to the saving knowledge of Jesus Christ, your Son. Bless them, O God. And bless those who hate us and persecute us. Save them, we pray. We do not pray for ourselves, but for those who do not know you as Lord and Savior. Bless them, O Lord Jesus, and bless Your holy Name".

You hear the cries from North Korea, as the family of the teenage girl martyred for her love of God's Word is making their requests known to God.

Prayers are also rising by the thousands from China... prayers of suffering Chinese believers lifting up their voices in one accord as they joyfully accept the plundering of their possessions. The smoke from their burning churches is rising to heaven along with their prayers...

"Do not lay this sin at their charge, O Lord... bless those who persecute us, and open their eyes, O God, to the Truth. May your Word find a place in their hearts this day... and may you receive great glory, Lord Jesus, our Rock, and our Redeemer".

Then all of a sudden a great rumbling begins across the western world.

"What's that sound?", you ask!

A roaring choir of voices is rising from the earth.
You look around and see that sorrow has overcome the faces of the saints on every side.

"It's the prayers rising to heaven from America," one of them explains.

And it is then that you are able to understand the dialogue of the mighty chorus, the thundering chant.

It is the voices of millions upon millions of Christians rising to heaven from the United States of America...

"BLESS ME, LORD... BLESS ME INDEED... BLESS ME..., BLESS ME A LOT!... BLESS ME...BLESS ME... BLESS ME... BLESS ME"!

The volume of the voices is so loud, and the chorus so overpowering that the prayers of the suffering persecuted believers across the rest of the world are drowned out by wave after wave of their incessant demands.

"What is this?" you ask- "What's going on?"

A man turns around and answers you. "It is the prayers of millions of Christians rising up from the wealthiest nation that has ever existed in all of history. God has given them so much, yet they still cry day and night for more."

"Little book... Big Lie"

An immensely popular book amongst Christians and non-believers alike, "The Prayer of Jabez" has recently swept the western world, selling millions of copies and topping charts all across America and Europe.

For nearly two months I heard one report after another of Christians who were raving about this little 93 page book.

I have been the pastor of a non-denominational Bible Church in a small town in Texas for many years, and have never seen such euphoria in the Christian community over any other teaching.

The reactions by professing believers to "The Prayer of Jabez" that I was hearing on a regular basis were both uniform and troublesome.

Christians who once prayed for those things dear to the heart of God were now convinced that they should pray for personal blessing. I watched as the Jabez fad swallowed up unsuspecting believers by the droves, diverting their attention from the proclamation of the Gospel and care of the poor, to a subtle, sometimes blatant, covetousness.

After reading the book myself I realized that I could no longer remain silent.

How could a small passage of Scripture be so misinterpreted, misunderstood, and misapplied by so many in such a short period of time?

It did not take long for me to figure it out. **"The Prayer of Jabez", by Bruce Wilkinson, is a book made for our time. It is a book written for a generation that seeks to benefit from a "little prayer with a giant prize", a generation of self-seeking believers who have lost sight of the "prize of the high calling of God in Christ Jesus". (Phillipians 3:14)**

All across the world believers in Christ are suffering in need of the basic necessities for daily survival. Yet while they are being persecuted and martyred for their faith in Jesus, millions of professing Christians in America and Europe covet a life of perpetual ease, and plenty.

Just listen to these word for word quotations from Wilkinson's Jabez books for adults, teens, and kids…

"Do you want to be extravagantly blessed by God?
...Pray the Jabez prayer every morning...
...only one sentence... tucked away in the Bible...
...it contains the key to a life of extra-ordinary favor with God...
...I prayed the little prayer myself – word for word...
...I've been praying Jabez for more than half my life...
...The Jabez prayer distills God's powerful will for your future...
...Follow unwaveringly the plan outlined here for the next thirty days...
...each of Jabez's requests can release something miraculous in your life...
...release God's favor, power, and protection...
...you can change your future...change what happens one minute from now...
...you will change your legacy and bring supernatural blessings wherever you go...
...supernatural blessing, influence, and power...
...little prayer... giant prize...
...bless me...and what I really mean is...bless me a lot!...
...nothing but God's fullest blessing will do...
...when you take little steps, you don't need God...
...thousands... are seeing miracles happen on a regular basis...
...your life will become marked by miracles...
...adventure, excitement, and lots of fun...
...it's the kind of life He promises each of us...
...an exciting way to live - being partners with God...
...His only limitation is us-when we don't ask...
... (be) not afraid to sound selfish...
... (be) willing to ask God for whatever (you) want...
...you want something bigger... something huge...
...such a prayer is not the self-centered act it might appear...
...God wants you to be selfish in your prayers...
...to ask for more, and more again...
...much , much more than you've ever thought to ask Him for...

...Lord, increase the value of my investment portfolios...
...you were redeemed for this: to ask Him for the God-sized best...
...we release God's power to accomplish His will...
...your want for God's plenty has been His will for your life from eternity past...
...seeking God's blessings is our ultimate act of worship...
...God will release His miraculous power in your life now. And for all eternity He will lavish on you His honor and delight"

(All of these quotes are referenced on pages 110 and 111 at the back of this book.)

It is frightening when one considers how many prominent Christian leaders have fallen prey to the "Jabez revolution", when even a casual *walk thru the Bible* reveals the error of these teachings.

Yet people of every religious persuasion, every denomination, and every theological background have accepted Wilkinson's new gospel. And I am convinced that unless the grave error of the teaching in his book, "The Prayer of Jabez", is refuted, this heresy will lay the foundation for even greater heresies in the near future.

The broad appeal of the book, "The Prayer of Jabez", can be attributed to the fact that the author preaches Christianity without cost, avoiding the message of the Cross altogether and completely.

There is no crucifixion, no death, no blood, no suffering, no trial of faith, no persecution, and in fact, not even a mention of Jesus until the book is nearly half finished. This sad reality has become a common characteristic of the best-selling pseudo-Christian and "religious" books of our time.

The message of the Cross, which speaks of faith, humility,

denial of self, and obedience unto death has been exchanged for a message of personal peace, prosperity, and affluence.

The message of the Cross is despised by the world. It will never sell millions of books in the midst of "an evil and adulterous generation". For it is "an evil and adulterous generation", Jesus says, that "seeketh after a sign". (Matthew 12:39)

We live in the midst of a culture that desires personal *"blessings... miracles on a regular basis... favor... success... (and) plenty"*, as Wilkinson promises the buyers of his Jabez books. Yet Jesus warned of trials, tribulation, persecution, and hatred for those who would be His disciples.

All who preach "Christ and Him crucified" are hated of the world, as Jesus said, "All men will hate you because of me", and, "If they persecuted me, they will persecute you". (John 15:20)

But "an evil and adulterous generation" wants a "Jabez" kind of life, not a "Jesus" kind of life.

Jesus Christ never sinned... yet He took upon Himself the sins of the world... He was stripped naked, beaten, bludgeoned, whipped and spat upon. His flesh was ripped from His body, His beard plucked out, and a crown of thorns forced into His skull. He was "marred beyond the visage of any man", as the prophet foretold. He was nailed to a wooden Cross and raised up that He might draw all men unto Himself. Jesus paid in full the price for our sins and all who believe on Him are reconciled to God and have eternal Life. This is the message of the Cross. All who would be disciples of Christ are called to take up their crosses and follow Him.

The Apostle Paul said that one could preach anything other than "the Cross of Christ" and not suffer persecution. **Those who preach Jabez will never suffer persecution.**

"Men of Jabez", as Wilkinson calls them, work from a position of strength, influence, and unlimited bounty. But men and women of God who share "Christ and Him crucified" identify more with the experience of the Apostle Paul...

"We are hard pressed on every side, yet not crushed; we are perplexed, but not in despair; persecuted, but not forsaken; struck down, but not destroyed; always carrying about in the body the dying of the Lord Jesus, that the Life of Jesus might also be manifested in our body." (II Corinthians 4:7-10)

"For Thy sake we are killed all the day long; we are accounted as sheep for the slaughter..." (Romans 8:36)

"... as the ministers of God, in much patience, in afflictions, in necessities, in distresses, in stripes, in imprisonments, in tumults, in labours, in watchings, in fastings,... as sorrowful, yet always rejoicing, as poor, yet making many rich, as having nothing, and yet possessing all things." (II Corinthians 6:4-10)

"For to <u>you</u> it has been granted on behalf of Christ, not only to believe in Him, but also to suffer for His sake."

(Phillipians 1:29)

2
Giants of the Faith

He was just a little boy, maybe nine or ten years old. I read about him in an ancient Christian history book written by a man named Eusebius. He lived with his parents in the city of Tyre in an area of the world known as Palestine.

His name was Ulpianus. But his mom and dad probably just called him "Ulpi". Like every boy his age I'm sure he loved to play. He probably worked in his father's trade as an apprentice like most of the youths of his day. His whole life was before him.

But times were tough for a Christian family living in Palestine in the year 301. You didn't just stand up in public and say "I am a believer in Jesus Christ" unless you had counted the cost, unless you really meant it. You did not meet on Sundays to play church. Anyone who professed faith in Jesus Christ was under threat of imprisonment and execution by the state. So Christianity was serious business.

At that time Palestine was under the authoritarian power of a tyrant by the name of Maximinus Ceasar. His hatred for "the sect of the Nazarene" was great. And in the eighteenth year of his reign, in the month of April, he began a general persecution. Thousands of Christian men, women, and children were tortured, drowned or burned at the stake by this dictator.

We all remember the names of great heroes from history. Patrick Henry, Alexander Graham Bell, and Louis Pasteur are all listed in the historical record for great deeds. Whether they fought for freedom, were great inventors, or made huge medical and scientific advances, we honor them as heroes from the past.

But in the world famous book "Who's Who" Ulpi is not listed. He is a nobody as far as modern historians are concerned. But in the Kingdom of God and in heaven he is a somebody.

Ulpi had seen the cruelty of this Ceasar on more than one occasion. He knew that the authorities were using every torture conceivable to force Christians to deny their Lord and sacrifice to the "gods" of Rome. Yet throughout the persecution Ulpi held *unswervingly* to his faith.

Many have denied Christ in times past for the mere sake of food or water. But this little boy was the real article. The horrors Ulpi witnessed against the church of Jesus only served to strengthen his resolve to suffer for the Name of Jesus.

Another youth from a neighboring town, a teenager, had just been martyred for interfering with the heathen sacrifice. This older boy had interrupted their idolatry by taking hold of the priests arm and declaring to the heathen crowds that there is but one God that men everywhere should obey (Keep in mind that their were no 'youth groups' to guide the teens in these early churches). The authorities immediately turned on the older youth beating him with blows over his entire body, and ripping his flesh to the bone. Strong men beat this teenage boy's face beyond recognition. Yet even after this brother in the Lord was skinned, burned with fire, and thrown into the sea, Ulpi made the same confession… faith in Jesus Christ.

He was immediately taken by soldiers, tortured and scourged. And when it was certain that the little boy would not deny Christ but would follow in the footsteps of his teenage mentor, the authorities enclosed him in a leather sack with a dog and a poisonous snake and threw him into the sea.

Ulpi died a violent and painful death for the "Crucified One".

"...(some) were tortured, not accepting deliverance,
that they might obtain a better resurrection.
Still others had trial of mockings and scourgings,
Yes, and of chains and imprisonment.
They were stoned, they were sawn in two,
Were tempted, were slain with the sword.
They wandered about in sheepskins,
Being destitute, afflicted, tormented-
Of whom the world is not worthy"

(Hebrews 11:35-38)

"First and Most"

In the popular book "The Prayer of Jabez", by Bruce Wilkinson, there is a chapter about *"Giants of the Faith"* in which the author attempts to convince the reader that there is one defining difference between *"great men... and the rest of us."* The difference, according to Wilkinson is simple... great men pray for themselves *"first and most"*, while ordinary men do not.

The reader is taken on a fictional journey to a *"spiritual retreat in the mountains"* where he learns that *"selfish"* prayers are *"exactly the kind of request our Father longs to hear"*.

I have never been so grieved by a "Christian" book as I was the day I read chapter two of "The Prayer of Jabez".

Wilkinson begins, *"You're at a spiritual retreat in the mountains with others who want to experience a fuller Christian life. For the duration of the retreat everyone has been matched with a mentor. Yours is in his seventies... On the way to the showers the first morning, you walk past his room. His door is ajar, and he has just knelt down to pray. You can't resist"*.

Wilkinson then has the reader eavesdrop on this *"giant of the faith"* as he begins his morning prayer... *"Will he pray for revival?" Does he "pray for the hungry around the world?" Will he "pray for you?"*

No, Wilkinson insists that a *"giant of the faith"* prays for himself, *"Oh Lord, I beg you first and most this morning please bless...me!"*

Wilkinson then takes the reader through the full gamut of emotions that the average believer feels after hearing such a selfish prayer. It appears that his aim is to destroy the God-given revulsion to this kind of selfish and fleshly praying by convincing the reader that it is neither.

Wilkinson goes on, *"Startled at such a selfish prayer, you pad down the hall to your shower."* The Holy Spirit has obviously convicted the reader by this point that something is terribly wrong with this old *"giant"*, and his prayer life too. So the rest of the author's fictional trapping is absolutely essential to sell the theme of his book.

So, says the author, *"you pad down the hall to your shower."* You are shocked. You are full of righteous indignation at the self-serving attitude of this uninspiring elder.

You expected to hear an older man of the faith pray humbly before God, like Jesus prayed in the garden of Gethsemane, **"Not my will, but Thine be done."** But instead you hear this self-centered old geezer sounding really spiritual while he's praying for himself. By now you're feeling kind of sick.

Then comes the curve. Wilkinson flaunts a new idea, a novel invention. Forget the example of Christ and the apostles. Forget everything you learned in Sunday School about praying for revival, food for the hungry, and those in need. Forget what the Bible says about denying yourself and taking up your cross daily. This is the twenty-first century, baby! You need to start *"Breaking through to the Blessed Life"*,says Wilkinson, and pray, *"first and foremost ... bless me".*

Wilkinson continues, *"But as you're adjusting the water temperature, a thought hits you. It's so obvious you can't believe you haven't thought it before. Great men of the faith think differently than the rest of us. The reason some men and women of faith rise above the rest is that they think and pray differently than those around them."*(From Chapter Two of "The Prayer of Jabez")

In other words, Wilkinson sees two distinct classes of believers; those who have figured out how to get their prayers answered by reciting an Old Testament prayer every morning, and those who have not. Those who figured it out, *"experience the life-changing effects of the Jabez prayer... (the) release of (God's) miraculous power, now and for all eternity... (and) rise above the rest."*

And those who do not, well... they just remain, in the words of Bruce Wilkinson, *"ordinary"*.

It's as if there was nothing before "The Prayer of Jabez" to this author. How Christianity could have survived for two millennia without uncovering the secret power of the Jabez prayer is inconceivable. After two thousand years of Christians praying like Jesus taught us in the Lord's Prayer, Wilkinson has discovered that, actually, it is *"the Jabez prayer (that) distills God's powerful will for your future."*

If only Ulpianus of Tyre and all of the other believers down through the ages martyred for their faith in Christ had known about *"the Jabez blessing"*, they would not have needed to suffer. If Bruce Wilkinson is right that, *"seeking God's blessings is our ultimate act of worship,"* then why lay down your life for Jesus Christ? The Lord really only wants you to make *"a lifelong commitment to ask God every day to bless you, and while He's at it, bless you a lot?"* After all, says Wilkinson, *"...it is God's plan for His most-honored servants".*

The author of the Jabez books has invented a very broad-

based and appealing message, but it is not associated with the Gospel of Jesus Christ.

Remember how in Acts Chapter Five Peter and the other apostles were beaten for their public preaching of Jesus? These men are our examples of *"God's most honored servants"*, and upon their release they went their way praising God that they had been counted worthy to suffer and be shamed for Jesus' sake. The Jabez books paint a picture of an American dream type Christianity where the most honored of God are daily blessed with *plenty* and *"make a lifelong commitment"* to ask God for more.

"God's plan for His most honored servants" is not necessarily a life of security, and ease, and plenty. If the Apostles are a good example of God's most honored servants, then one might conclude that God's plan for his most honored servants is martyrdom.

Weak and foolish

In his chapter entitled *"The Touch of Greatness"* Wilkinson recounts how he is impressed by a group of teenagers who took his advice and began to pray, *"Lord, please bless us."* He then attributes their success in ministry to their diligence at praying the first two elements of the Jabez prayer.

How any Christian man could encourage young people, teenagers, and even little children (Jabez for Teens/Jabez for Kids /Jabez for Little Ones) to *"…follow unwaveringly the plan outlined here* (in his Jabez books) *for the next thirty days"*, promising *"supernatural blessing, influence, and power… adventure, excitement, and fun"* in return is beyond me. It is not only silly, it is also heresy.

At a men's prayer meeting at our church recently many of the men were down on their knees praying while others lay prostrate on their faces before God. Several young boys had gathered in front of the altar and were on their knees praying along with their fathers. After the men finished praying, one by one these young boys ages six, seven, and eight began to pray.

They did not pray for personal blessings. In fact, they did not pray for themselves at all.

They prayed for the poor children in Mexico they had seen when our church took food and clothing along with Spanish Bibles into a colonia, a small village where whole families lived in cardboard and pallet houses eating the refuse brought in by garbage trucks from the city of Matamoros.

They prayed for the poor, persecuted peoples of Southern Sudan in Africa where many children have been kidnapped from their mommies and daddies to be used as sex slaves by Muslim soldiers.

They went on to pray for their own mothers and ailing grandmothers, believing that God in heaven hears the prayers of little ones who put their trust in Him.

Were their tender little hearts in the wrong place? Is Jesus ashamed of them because their hearts were broken for the hungry, suffering, and persecuted of our world today? Would Christ have been more pleased if they had prayed for personal blessings?

Their prayers did not fit in with the popular trend, the modern self centered petitions of the Jabez cult. Many of the popular Jabez teachers today would exhort our church leadership to rebuke these children who pray in such a way, *"Teach them to pray a prayer the Father loves to hear... Bless Me Lord, Bless Me Indeed"*.

But I say these teachers would do well to remember the words of Christ in the eighteenth chapter of Matthew, **"except ye be converted and become as little children, ye shall not enter into the kingdom of heaven,"** and **"take heed that ye despise not one of these little ones for I say unto you that in heaven their angels do always behold the face of My Father which is in heaven."**

Growing up as a youth in the church I was always taught that God used young men like David to slay giants. God used small armies, like Gideon's little band, to route and destroy armies of over a hundred thousand. I was taught that God has never really needed *"giants of the faith"* to accomplish his purposes in the earth.

God seems to be more interested in using those of a humble and contrite spirit, as it is written in the Scriptures, **"a broken and contrite heart, O God, thou wilt not despise."** (Psalm 51:17)

He seems to use those poor unknown nobodies like John the Baptist, who was clothed in camel's hair, and existed on a diet of locusts and wild honey… and poor fishermen like Peter and Andrew, who immediately dropped their nets when called to follow Jesus.

And yes, I believe, little boys too, who pray not for themselves, but for others in need.

God help believers in our rich American churches to repent of their self-centered prayer life and materialistic mentality, and return to that which is dear to the heart of God. Yes, God help us, and grant us repentance, in the Name of Jesus Christ.

"...not many mighty, not many noble are called. But God hath <u>chosen the foolish</u> things of the world to confound the wise; and God hath <u>chosen the weak</u> things of the world to confound the things which are mighty; and base things of the world, and things which are despised, hath God chosen, yea, and things which are not, to bring to nought (nothing) the things that are: That no flesh should glory in His presence".

(1Corinthians 1:27)

3
"Bruce, and the
gospel of Jabez"

One night after reading several chapters in the book of Acts, you nod off to sleep and begin to dream. In your dream you realize that you are standing in the streets of Jerusalem. It's the day of Pentecost, and the crowds are huge. People from all of the surrounding countries are gathering in the streets for the celebrations.

It has not been long since Christ ascended into the heavens in a cloud, and everyone is talking about the many strange things they have both seen and heard. What a great dream!

As you are wading through the crowds you notice that a commotion has begun at the house where someone said the followers of the man Jesus are meeting.

It is 9 a.m. in the morning and the disciples of Christ have just heard the sound of a rushing mighty wind coming from heaven. They are all filled with the Holy Spirit and people from every nation who are gathered there at Jerusalem hear the apostles speaking in their own language "the wonderful works of God". You hear the words of the apostles, also, and wish that it was not just a dream. You hope that you never wake up.

Almost immediately you see the apostle Peter standing up before the crowd of people and gesturing with his hands for silence as he begins to speak…

"This is that which was spoken of by the prophet Joel; 'And it shall come to pass in the last days, saith God, I will pour out my Spirit upon all flesh: and your sons and your daughters shall prophesy, and your young men shall see visions, and your old men shall dream dreams... and I will shew wonders in the heavens above, and signs in the earth beneath; blood, and fire, and vapour of smoke... The sun shall be turned into darkness, and the moon into blood, before that great and notable day of the Lord come...And it shall come to pass, that whosoever shall call upon the Name of the Lord shall be saved."

Peter's message is very clear. He is calling the nations to repentance and faith in Jesus Christ. As Peter continues to preach you see expressions of deep conviction on the faces of the people all around you.

"God hath made that same Jesus, whom ye have crucified, both Lord and Christ...save yourselves from this untoward (crooked) generation."

Many around you begin to cry. Others are kneeling and praying. The convicting power of the Holy Spirit sweeps through the crowd like a fire!

The Bible says in the second chapter of Acts that "fear came upon every soul: and many wonders and signs were done by the apostles". Three thousand souls were saved that day as Peter preached Jesus Christ, crucified and risen from the dead.

As you are listening you begin to wonder why so little of this kind of simple, yet powerful, preaching is not being heard in the modern day and time.

But just as you are pondering the thought, a commotion begins back behind you. You turn and look up above the heads of the crowds to see that another man has stood up and is preaching to the people from a balcony opposite of Peter and the apostles.

You hear a lady behind you say, **"His name is Bruce, and he has a different message. He says he has discovered** *'the key to a life of extra-ordinary favor with God'*. He has a little book that he is selling, and he promises everyone *'supernatural'* power from God in their lives if they will pray an Old Testament prayer for thirty days that was once prayed by a man named Jabez." You notice that people are beginning to move away from Peter, who is preaching Christ and Him crucified, and gravitating towards the Jabez preacher.

Bruce begins to speak, and you can't believe what you are hearing.

He says that he has discovered *"a daring prayer that God always answers... one sentence... tucked away in the Bible,"* and that thousands, who pray it every day for thirty days and longer, *"are seeing miracles happen on a regular basis"*. Has he uncovered a truth that Bible teachers and scholars have missed for hundreds of years?

Bruce continues, *"The Jabez prayer distills God's powerful will for your future... you can change your future... you can change what happens one minute from now...pray the Jabez prayer every morning... it's only what you believe will happen and therefore do next that will release God's power... you will change your legacy and bring supernatural blessings wherever you go... experience the life-changing effects of the Jabez prayer"*. **(Remember that all words in italics are direct quotes from Bruce Wilkinson's Jabez books for adults, teens, and kids!)**

You are horrified. You cannot believe that anyone could preach such a thing.

The message of Jabez is not *"life-changing"*, as this guy is claiming. Only the Gospel of Jesus Christ is *"life-changing"*. The prayer of Jabez is not a *"prayer that God always answers"*. A prayer of repentance and faith in the finished work of Christ on the cross is the only *"prayer that God always answers"*.

"This man is preaching lies to the people in the name of God," you think.

But Bruce continues to sell his Jabez books, *"Who wants a life that's just plain ordinary? Wouldn't you rather have one that's filled with adventure, excitement, and lots of fun? Well, as it turns out, that's just the kind of life God wants for you, too. And it's the kind of life He promises each of us… it's an exciting way to live, being partners with God."*(pages 1 and 84, Wilkinson's *"Jabez for Kids"* book)

"Fun, excitement, adventure… being partner's with God?', you think to yourself, "Where is this guy coming from? He's twisting and perverting the right ways, and turning people away from the Faith…"

Almost immediately you awaken. In a cold sweat you thank God that it was all just a bad dream.

But then you realize that your bad dream is actually a nightmare of reality. The Bible says that Jesus Christ is the same, yesterday, today, and forever. Time does not make a lie become truth, just as time does not make life evolve from inorganic matter.

If Bruce's gospel would have been a false and misleading message on the day of Pentecost, then it is a false and misleading message today. You shudder to think that millions upon millions of people in the United States have read Bruce's books and hung their hopes on a false teaching.

But this is nothing new. False teachers have been leading people away from the truth since the beginning. In fact you remember the place in the book of Acts where the Apostle Paul dealt with a similar distraction from the Gospel. You had just read it before falling asleep, and the Bible is still lying there opened to the very page in Chapter Thirteen.

Paul and Barnabas were preaching the Word of God in the synagogues of the Jews. But when the deputy of the country, Sergius Paulus, called for them to come and preach the Word to him, a false prophet named Bar-Jesus, sought to turn away the deputy from the faith.

Bar-Jesus, the Bible tells us, was also known as Elymas, the sorcerer, which is his name by interpretation.

But Paul recognized the deceitful message of Bar-Jesus, how his words were perverting the Word of God, and dealt with him swiftly.

"O full of all subtilty and all mischief, thou child of the devil, thou enemy of all righteousness, wilt thou not cease to pervert the right ways of the Lord? And now, behold, the hand of the Lord is upon thee, and thou shalt be blind, not seeing the sun for a season…"

Paul judged Bar-Jesus on the spot and sentenced him to temporary blindness, and this sorcerer went away "seeking someone to lead him by the hand".

I want to make something very clear to the reader of this book right now:

The message of Bruce Wilkinson's book, "The Prayer of Jabez", (not the Old Testament prayer itself), **is a message of sorcery.**

The belief in the power of the recitation of words, or prayers, is a cornerstone of the occultic teachings of witchcraft and sorcery. The practice is known as "incantation".

Jesus strictly forbade the praying of prayers word for word, yet

Wilkinson has taught his followers to do exactly that.

Jesus said, "When ye pray, <u>use not vain repetitions</u>, as the heathens do: for they think they shall be heard for their much speaking." He then goes on to tell us how we are to pray, "After this manner therefore pray ye", and the Lord's Prayer follows. Jesus condemns *"word for word"* repetition of prayers as something that "heathens" do. He then tells us how to pray, not what to pray.

Wilkinson says, when you pray, *"Pray the Jabez prayer every morning"* (vain repetitions). He then gives testimonials of several successful men, one of whom is a heart surgeon, who claim that they have been *"praying Jabez"* for many years with fantastic *"results"*. But Wilkinson cuts them short, *"Friends, I've been praying Jabez for more than half my life"*. Bruce Wilkinson claims that he has prayed for more than thirty years, the prayer that Jabez is recorded to have prayed only once!

Another strong tenet of sorcery and witchcraft is the teaching that one can *"change what happens one minute from now"* by reciting certain elements of a prayer or incantation. Some Jabez preachers are now admonishing their flocks to pray "The Prayer of Jabez" seventy and eighty times a day. After all, if the prayer Jabez prayed is *"a supremely spiritual one, and just the kind of request our Father longs to hear"*, as Wilkinson preaches, then the more you recite it the more *"our Father"* must be pleased.

But if, as Jesus says, the repetition of prayers is a heathen custom that God is not pleased with, then one must wonder what *"Father"* Wilkinson is pleasing. Nowhere in Scripture do we find anyone, not even Jabez himself, who was ever recorded as having prayed the prayer of Jabez every day.

The teaching of Bruce Wilkinson, that men, women, and children everywhere should *"Pray the Jabez prayer every morning"*, **as it says on page 86 of his book, is in direct**

violation of Jesus' commandment concerning prayer. And that which is in direct violation of Jesus' teaching is pleasing only to the devil.

Jesus said that if one could not hear or accept His Word that it was because "ye are of your father, the devil", in whom there is no truth, "When he speaketh a lie, he speaketh of his own: for he is a liar, and the father of it…he that is of God heareth God's words: ye therefore hear them not, because ye are not of God." In other words, those who hear and accept what Jesus says in His Word are known to be of their Father in heaven, but those who cannot receive it are of their father, the devil.

Wilkinson's doctrine is far, far from New Testament orthodoxy. The elements of his Jabez teachings, as I have just said, can be found readily, however, in the occult, in witchcraft, and in eastern religious practices.

In fact, about the same time that "The Prayer of Jabez" was released to Christians in America, another little book, with similar teachings, was being flaunted by the well known Tibetan Buddhist monk, The Dalai Lama.

Notice the similarities in the teachings below:

"To recite the Medicine Buddha Mantra brings inconceivable merit…"- (to recite the prayer of Jabez *"brings supernatural blessings"*).

"If you recite the Mantra every day, the Buddhas and Bodhisattvas will always pay attention to you, and they will guide you…", says the Buddhist monk. (If you recite the prayer of Jabez *"every day for thirty days… God will release His miraculous power in your life… now… and for all eternity. He will lavish on you his honor and delight."*)

The apostle Paul warned us in advance that false teachers would depart from, or move away from, the truths of Scripture. In I Timothy, chapter four, verse one he says, "... **in the latter times some shall depart from the faith, giving heed to seducing spirits, and doctrines of devils... speaking lies, having their conscience seared with a hot iron**".

Through the teachings found in Bruce Wilkinson's "The Prayer of Jabez" Satan has introduced millions of Christians to "doctrines of devils" found in the manuals of witchcraft and Tibetan Buddhism. As believers give heed to these seducing spirits the groundwork is being laid for even greater deceptions in the near future. The last of these deceptions will be the greatest as false Christs and false prophets rise to super stardom performing "signs and wonders, to seduce, if it were possible, even the elect." (Mark 13:22)

In 2 Timothy, chapter four, and verse three he says, "**...the time will come when they will not endure (or accept) sound doctrine; but after their own lusts (desires) shall they heap to themselves teachers, having itching ears; And they shall turn away their ears from the truth, and shall be turned unto fables.**"

Friends, the time that Paul spoke about 2000 years ago is now upon us. Please do not be one of those of whom it was prophesied "**...shall turn away their ears from the Truth...**"

False teachings are accelerating rapidly and weaving their way into the very fabric of Christian life and doctrine. Each day that these teachings find new disciples in the churches of our land, Christians are becoming less and less effective in the world for Christ.

My prayer, at this moment, is that the Lord Jesus will open the eyes of millions to the Truth of His Word, that those who have been deceived might return to the Faith, which is in Christ Jesus alone, no longer to be carried away by "every wind of doctrine".

I plead with you this hour to seek the Lord with your whole heart; not to pray some Old Testament prayer over and over again, word for word, day after day; but to be grounded in the Scriptures. Consume God's Word on a daily basis. Seek His face and His will for your life morning by morning. And may the Lord, our God grant that you may be able, by His Word and by His Spirit, to discern the truth from the many lies being sold to God's people in these last days.

"I marvel that ye are so soon removed from Him that called you into the grace of Christ unto another (a different) gospel: which is not another: but there be some that trouble you, and would pervert the Gospel of Christ...

Having the understanding darkened, being alienated from the life of God through the ignorance that is in them, because of the blindness of their heart...

...henceforth be no more children, tossed to and fro, and carried about with every wind of doctrine...
...And be not conformed to this world: but be ye transformed by the renewing

of your mind, that ye may prove what is that good, and acceptable, and perfect, will of God."

(Galatians 1:6-7, Ephesians 4:18, 4:14, Roman 12:2)

4

More Honorable...

He was sitting at one of those big half circle booths at Denny's Restaurant with the rest of the guys finishing his pancakes and eggs when a scantily clad young woman walked by. It was one of those Thursday morning men's prayer breakfasts where several of the men of his church were enjoying an hour of prayer, feasting and fellowship. But without thought or hesitation, the eyes of each man at the table traced the girl's every move until she was out of view. As she passed from sight one of the men noticed that just beyond the girl, sitting in another half circle booth, were several older women from their church... watching them... watching her.

How low he felt as he realized what these older women of the church must be thinking. It was the kind of sickening feeling that makes a grown man want to crawl under a rock and hide. But it was too late now. There was nothing he could say or do to change what had just happened. And there was nothing he could say or do to change the perception of the older women of the church.

And what if he could change their perception. What if he could come up with some brilliant excuse for his behavior? What if he could say something that would cause him to come away from it all looking somewhat respectable? Would that really change anything?

He felt two feet tall. He wished he had not even shown up for the breakfast that morning.

But as the thoughts raced through his head he realized that the problem was not what the women of the church might be thinking about him, but what was God in heaven thinking about him right now? To think only of how the women of the church might now regard him, was pure hypocrisy.

How he wished that he could have it all to do over again. He would look the other way as the girl passed by. He would restrain his eyes from that lustful gaze. Instead of following after the flesh, he would follow after the Spirit.

But the die was cast. All he could do now is confess his waywardness, humble himself before the Lord, turning away from that which grieves the Holy Spirit so, and go forward in obedience.

But wait a minute. What if one of the men at the prayer breakfast had stood out in the crowd? What if one of the men had not studied the scantily clad young woman as she passed? What if one of them had restrained his eyes? Does not the same God who takes notice of those who are less honorable also take notice of those who are *"more honorable"*?

As they all bowed their heads in prayer at that big half-circle table at Denny's, whose prayer do you think God would have been more attentive to... the men who had made a hobby of feasting with their eyes upon the bodies of young scantily dressed women... or the man who, for the love of God, practiced righteousness?

The Apostle Peter answered this question well when he said, "...the eyes of the Lord are over the righteous, and <u>His ears are open to their prayers</u>, but the face of the Lord is set against them that do evil". (1 Peter 3:12) It is interesting to note that Peter's letter was not addressed to "them that do evil". Peter's letter was written to believers.

Yes, the answer is very clear. Our manner of life has much to do with the power and relevance of our prayers before God.

Yet there are many in our churches today who have gone far beyond the lustful gaze. Internet pornography, television, magazines, movies, and videos provide a steady diet of filth and impurity to many "Christian" homes across our land. Where once lived godly men in holy fear before the Lord, now reside "porno-freaks", who with the click of a mouse or remote control set a course to destroy their homes, marriages, and souls bowing in sexual worship to prostitutes and whores.

Men who once slew giants in the world for Christ are now being slain themselves by electronic images, paper, and ink. Until a man is serious enough about dealing with the dishonorable elements of his life, that he sets out to remove every wicked influence from before his eyes, he will not overcome the Evil One in this arena.

If access to the internet brings you to your knees before the altar of lust you must remove the computer from your home or office! If television brings the images of alluring and "scantily clad" women into your home then disconnect from the cable or antenna that allows it to enter! Whatever it is in your life that brings you continually to your knees to do the pleasure of the Evil One, rather than the Holy One, must be overthrown! You cannot live an honorable life before God while refusing to rid your home of wicked and evil influences.

In the Bible there is a man who lived in the land of Uz whose name was Job. And according to the Word of God, **"that man was perfect, and upright, and one that feared God, and eschewed (avoided, turned away from) evil."** In the book of Job we find that this godly man made "a covenant" with his eyes not to look upon a woman with lust, knowing that God Almighty brings destruction on all who do. "Is it not destruction to the wicked, and a strange punishment to the workers of iniquity… doth not He (God) see my ways?". Job knew the answers to these questions, and he feared God.

Then one day, when "the sons of God came to present themselves before the Lord", Satan came too. **And the Lord said to Satan, "Hast thou considered my servant Job... there is none like him in the earth..."**

God notices! God cares. Wouldn't it be awesome to find out one day that God spoke of you in such a way... "there is none like him in all the earth"? Can you understand that God singles men out who fear Him and obey Him? The Bible is full of stories of good and obedient men and women who were "more honorable" than their brethren. And these men and women were used of God in many mighty ways. And their prayers were heard by the Lord!

"The prayer of the upright is His delight" (Proverbs 15:8) The prayer does not make the one who prays it upright. It is the one who is upright that makes the prayer, "His delight". God is delighted with the prayers of the upright, but, **"He that turneth away his ear from hearing the law, even his prayer shall be abomination".** (Proverbs 28:9)

And just as men are so often carried away by the tides of sexual immorality, so are many wives living in rebellion against God, being the "lord" of their homes.

In 1 Peter, Chapter Three, the apostle instructs the older women to teach the younger women to **"be sober, to love their husbands, to love their children, to be discreet, chaste, keeper's at home, good, obedient to their own husbands, that the word of God be not blasphemed".**

Many Christian women today cannot understand why God does not seem to hear their prayers. They become bitter and disillusioned after years of praying with seemingly little response from heaven. Yet all the while they resist the very change in their lives that would set them apart as *"more honorable"* in the sight of God. They have continually heard the

Word, but failed to take it to heart.

"Wives, submit to your own husbands as unto the Lord…

"…ye wives be in subjection to your own husbands; that if any obey not the Word, they also without the word may be won… for after this manner in the old time the holy women also, who trusted in God, adorned themselves, being in subjection unto their own husbands: even as Sarah obeyed Abraham, calling him lord…" (Ephesians 5:22, 1 Peter 3:1,5,6)

In all of my counseling sessions with couples over the years these two marital problems have arisen as the cause of more damage and division than all the others combined.

Mental adultery and insubmission reign as the leading causes of marital strife and division within the churches of America today. And as a result the prayer lives of so many a Christian couple are powerless as these sins wreak daily havoc and destruction. If there were a satanic manifesto for the collapse of Christian marriages, lust and insubmission would be found on page one.

 Satan knows that the Word of God is true… that Christian husbands and wives are, **"…heirs together of the grace of life…"**, as the Scriptures declare in 1 Peter, Chapter Three. He knows that when there is sin in a marriage that has not been dealt with (confessed to God and forsaken) that the prayers of the husband and wife are **"hindered"**.

But the Word of God says in Proverbs 16:17 that, **"The highway of the righteous is to depart from evil"**. We can choose to continue in our rebellion, spinning our wheels as they say, without much hope of fulfilling God's plan for our lives, living in ways that are not pleasing in the sight of God. Or we can seek God with our whole heart to trust and obey. It is really a choice that is set before us each and every day. We can fool ourselves into believing that God doesn't really notice, and so go on in lives of fruitlessness, being unproductive for the Kingdom of God, or we can believe the Word of God is true when it says that **"The effectual fervent prayer of a righteous man availeth much"**. (James 5:16)

The Request of Joe Smith

In Bruce Wilkinson's *"The Prayer of Jabez"* the author seems to labor over a question that plagues his mind. He desperately seeks for an answer to the question… **Why did God answer Jabez's prayer?** *"What was the secret…,"* Wilkinson asks. What *"secret"* did this guy know that caused him to get his prayer answered? Why did the writer of 1 Chronicles stop midstream in a list of genealogies to tell us about this unknown Old Testament figure named Jabez?

Wilkinson is perplexed.

But just as quickly as he asks the question, Wilkinson is convinced that he has found the answer. *"Clearly,"* says Wilkinson, *"Clearly, the outcome can be traced to his prayer… Something about Jabez's simple direct request to God changed his life…He prayed an unusual one –sentence prayer (and) things turned out extraordinarily well."*

Wilkinson completely misses the point. It was not *"an unusual one-sentence prayer"* that moved God to grant the request of Jabez. Yet the truth is so obvious that it seems one would trip over it. "Why did God answer Jabez's prayer? Let me quote the answer directly from *"The Prayer of Jabez"* as it is found in Wilkinson's book…

"Now Jabez was more honorable than his brothers...

...So God granted him what he requested."

In between these two sentences lies only the definition of Jabez's name, which is interpreted "Pain", and the list of his requests to God. The fact that Jabez led a more honorable life than all of his "brethren" of Israel is the reason why his prayers were answered. It's obvious.

Let me give you an illustration to make the point more clear. First the teenager's version:

"Now Bobby was more trustworthy than his brothers... so his parents let him go on a camping trip with his friends." Bobby's brothers asked if they could go camping, too, but because they were not as trustworthy as Bobby, they didn't get what they requested.

It didn't matter how they asked, even if they had said, "Pretty please, with sugar on it," it wouldn't have mattered. Bobby's brothers could not be trusted, and therefore their pleadings went unanswered (actually they *were* answered, and the answer was... "NO!")

Adult version: We'll call it **"The Request of Joe Smith."**

A man named Joe Smith applied for a job as a chemist at Dupont. The hiring office of the company takes one look at his qualifications for the job and hires him. The next day the company log reads...

"Now Joe Smith was more qualified than all of the other applicants... So the hiring office gave him the job he requested."

It was not the words Joe used to ask for the job that got him hired. It was the fact that "Joe Smith was more qualified" than his brethren.

Now let's go deeper into **"The Request of Joe Smith"** to emphasize this point:

"Now Joe Smith was more qualified than all of the other applicants...

And Joe Smith called the head of the hiring office saying...

'Oh that you would hire me indeed... and give me a big pay increase... and that you would always favor me on the job... and keep me from getting fired... that I might not default on my house and car payments.'

... So the hiring office gave him the job he requested."

Joe's four requests; to be hired, to be given a big pay increase, to be favored on the job, and to be kept from getting fired so that he wouldn't default on his loans, had nothing at all to do with his request being answered.

Joe was hired because **"Joe Smith was more qualified than all of the other applicants."**

Joe's request to be hired was not "just the kind of request the hiring office loved to hear." Dozens of applicants were asking the hiring office for that job every day. Requests for the position Joe got came in on a regular basis. There was no *"secret"* in the way that he asked. Joe was just "more qualified" than *"his brethren."*

In the same way, the Jabez prayer is no *"unusual"* prayer. There is no *"secret"* hidden in Jabez's words. There is no magic, no power, and no *"favor"* with God granted because one recites certain words. God is not *"delighted"* with vain repetitions, as

Wilkinson insists. Jabez's prayer is no exalted incantation. Jabez's prayer was answered for one reason, and one reason only:

"Jabez was more honorable than his brethren."

Joe's colleagues could have asked Dupont for the job from sunrise to sunset and they never would have been hired. His "brethren" could have recited "**The Request of Joe**" *"word for word… every day for thirty days"* and seen no change in their employment status.

In the same way, Jabez's brothers could have prayed the prayer that Jabez prayed until they were blue in the face, and they would not have moved God's hand at all.

On the other hand, Jabez could have prayed for anything in line with God's will and it would have been granted. **It was not the prayer that was significant, but the life of the one who prayed the prayer, and the fact that his prayer was in line with the will of God for his life!**

Let's look at a Biblical example of what I am saying.

In the book of Daniel in the Bible we find the prophet kneeling down "as was his custom" to fast and to pray "to the God of heaven". After fasting and praying for fourteen days, an angel appears and tells Daniel that his request has been granted. In fact, the angel declares that Daniels prayer was answered the first day that he began to fast and pray! God was not impressed with the eloquent words of Daniel's prayer. God was impressed with Daniel's life.

God knew Daniel's heart. And Daniel's heart was consistent with his honorable manner of living. He not only talked the talk, but he also walked the walk.

But many Christians today want God to hear their prayers even when they are living in known sin. Millions pray the same words that Jabez prayed, but few live honorably before God.

Honoring God with your lips, and honoring God with the obedience and reverence of holy living are two different things.

"This people draw nigh (near) unto me with their mouth, and honoureth me with their lips; but their heart is far from me."

(Isaiah 29:13)

5
Treasure in Heaven

Many are convinced that an increase in wealth is a sign that God is pleased with the way they are living. When things are going well and the money is flowing they assume that it is the direct result of their "goodness", and an indication of God's great pleasure with all that they are doing.

But there is a danger in this type of thinking. It is a flawed theology that teaches believers that a life of plenty is God's way of saying, "Well done, good and faithful servant."

I'll use Hugh Hefner, the wealthy pornographer who built the huge "Playboy" empire, as an example. If the advent of money and "success" is a sign of heaven's favor, then this man would be the classic example of a saint.

As it turns out, though, Hefner is a lost, degenerate, and miserable soul who has built his fortune on the sexual exploitation of other men's wives and daughters. His enterprise of evil has destroyed untold millions of lives around the world. Wealthy pornographers, like Hefner, have prostituted countless young women for profit, causing the destruction of many Christian and non-Christian homes in the process. Many of his "patrons" have gone on to become notorious rapists and child molestors.

Another not so shining example of the apparently "successful" of our time would be the host of "television evangelists" who have extorted millions of dollars from their hopeful, yet Biblically shallow, followers. Promising "miracles…. healing… and financial success" to those who "sowed" into their "ministries", these self proclaimed prophets, "subvert whole houses, teaching things they ought not", for the sake of monetary gain. Their "ministries" have been very "successful" by this world's standards. Yet, these so-called "preachers of the Gospel" have become extravagantly rich in the Christian marketplace.

In the 1980's several prime time television "ministries" crashed and burned before the eyes of the world. Adultery, homosexuality, embezzlement, and misappropriation of funds by these false teachers caused the "...Word of God to be evil spoken of...", and "...blasphemed among the heathen".

So I ask you, were these men "blessed of God"? Was their success and accumulation of wealth from the hand of God? I think not. Scandal after scandal ensued leaving a wake of hurting, disoriented, and discouraged believers. The damage done by these so-called "ministries" was incalculable, laying waste entire congregations and churches here and abroad.

Do not be deceived. Satan will use any and every means at his disposal to pervert, subvert, and discredit the Word of God.

Financial well being is not necessarily a sign of God's great pleasure with the life of any person.

Richard Wurmbrand spent fourteen years in a prison in communist Romania beginning in 1948. His life was one of poverty. He was tortured often while in chains for the Gospel and spent three years in solitary confinement thirty feet underground.

His wife, Sabina, spent ten years in prison for her efforts to spread the Good News of the saving grace of Jesus. Upon her arrest in 1950 the Wurmbrand's nine year old son was left alone on the streets until an elderly widow took him in and cared for him.

Sometime after their release from prison the Wurmbrands came to the United States and started a ministry to persecuted brothers and sisters in the Lord across the globe. Their organization, Voice of the Martyrs, has sent hundreds of thousands of Bibles and tracts, crates of food and clothing, along with other necessities to persecuted Christians in every part of the world.

In the year 2000 both Richard and Sabina went on to be with the Lord. He was ninety-one years old, and she was eighty-nine.

Unlike the "abundant life", and "bless me" ministries of the modern era, the Wurmbrand's ministry was administered modestly. As long as they lived on earth they never owned a home or automobile of their own. But they were indeed *blessed* of the Lord.

Our church helps support the preaching tours of a traveling evangelist named Jim Phillips. You have probably never heard of him. Homeless men at the Salvation Army have heard of him. People on the streets of many cities have heard him preach, though they do not know him by name.

In Mexico he has traveled unknown, preaching the Gospel of Jesus Christ to thousands.

One cold and rainy winter day a couple of years ago Jim called me and told me he believed God wanted him to go and preach on the streets of a neighboring central Texas town. I met him at the church in Burnet, we prayed, and Jim went off into the freezing rain to share Christ with anyone who would listen.

Standing on the public sidewalk in front of the post office he spoke to the people, Bible in hand. He was speaking through a small plastic cone, like those you see used by cheerleaders at football games.

Officers from the local Police Department were dispatched immediately, and upon hearing his message they asked Jim to leave their city. They then escorted him to the city limit sign and he left town.

Jesus was once escorted to the city limit sign, too. He had mercy on a wild man "living in the tombs" that was very violent and possessed with demons. But after casting the demon out and restoring the man to instant sanity the local authorities kicked Jesus out of town.

Jesus told his disciples to preach everywhere. But He warned that it would be **more tolerable for Sodom and Gomorrah on the day of judgment**", than for a city that rejected the Good News.

When Jim was just a little boy he got a thorn stuck in his eye and was partially blinded. I had noticed that one of the lenses of his glasses was a little cloudy at times, but I did not know of his handicap until just recently. But that's just the way Jim is. He would never seek compassion or pity for himself. I have never heard him complain about anything as long as I have known him. He has slept on church members' sofas, in gymnasiums, in sleeping bags, and on cots at homeless shelters.

Jim works as a delivery driver in Fort Worth, Texas to fund his preaching tours. With the money he saves from making deliveries and the support of a handful of believers he preaches the Gospel on the streets from Canada to Mexico.

He drives a 1992 Ford Ranger single cab pickup truck with nearly 200,000 miles on it. As I write Jim is in Mexico preaching across the interior. He is fluent in Spanish and draws crowds with his portable battery powered P.A. system.

The men of our church tried to fix Jim's air-conditioning on his truck one Sunday after church. The hundred degree plus weather in Mexico can be very dangerous, and we wanted him to have at least some occasional relief available.

But even after installing a new compressor, clutch, and accumulator we failed to get anything but a steady stream of hot air from the inside vents. Yet when the men of the church offered to order more parts to fix the system on Monday, Jim declined. He was sure that God would have him preaching the next day on the sun-scorched streets of Nuevo Laredo... a/c or not.

Jim is in his 50's. Yet at an age when most men are thinking about retirement, he is still thinking about the **"prize of the high calling of God in Christ Jesus"**. Jim does not own a home here on earth. Years ago he received a large inheritance after the death of a relative and could have bought a nice home to retire in. But instead Jim gave it all away.

When one of the ladies from our church told me how Jim had twice given away all his earthly possessions to follow Jesus, I was immediately reminded of the place in the Bible where Jesus talked about true wealth... treasure in heaven.

As the story goes, a rich young ruler had asked Jesus what he needed to do to inherit eternal life. Jesus told the youth to keep the commandments. The young man claimed that he had kept them all since he was just a boy (claiming to be "good" when Jesus had just told him that God alone was good). When the youth pressed the question further Jesus offered the young man great wealth...

"If thou wilt be perfect, go and sell what thou hast, and give to the poor, and thou shalt have treasure in heaven: and come follow me". At this the young ruler "went away sorrowful, for he had great possessions".

"Verily I say unto you... that a rich man shall hardly enter into the kingdom of heaven... it is easier for a camel to go through the eye of a needle, than for a rich man to enter into the kingdom of God". (Matthew 19:23-24)

As of the writing of this chapter I have not heard from Jim, but we are praying for God's blessing on his efforts as he suffers for the cause of Christ in a foreign land.

Little white fables

In Bruce Wilkinson's popular book, The Prayer of Jabez, there is a *"little fable"* about a man named Mr. Jones who goes to heaven. When he gets there he is taken on a tour by St. Peter to see all of the mansions and golden streets, but his attention is diverted to a building that looks like a big warehouse. Once inside Peter reluctantly allows Mr. Jones to open a white box on the "J" isle with his name on it. Inside the box are *"all the blessings that God wanted to give to him while he was still on earth... but Mr. Jones had never asked."* Of course Mr. Jones is very sad that he hadn't begged God to bless him every day while he was on earth.

The childish story is meant to motivate you, the believer, while still here on earth *"to ask God every day to bless you- and while He's at it, to bless you a lot"*(Chapter Two, Pages 28-29).

The *"fable"*, as Wilkinson calls it, attempts to reverse the Christ-centered objective of the believer here on earth. Instead of Jesus' teaching that we should be laying up for ourselves "treasure in heaven", Wilkinson teaches a retrospective outlook from heaven where one regrets not having laid up for himself "treasures on earth". *"...if you didn't ask Him for a blessing yesterday, you didn't get all you were supposed to have"*, Wilkinson goes on, *"If Jabez had worked on Wall Street, he might have prayed, Lord, increase the value of my investment portfolios."* It is a very cleverly devised fable indeed, a cunning sales pitch for a new "Christian" fad. But it is also a perversion of God's Word.

If Wilkinson had wanted to learn about *"fables"* and the teachings of St. Peter he need only have gone to the Word of God itself.

The Apostle Peter was very clear concerning these things, **"We have not followed cunningly devised fables when we made known unto you the coming and power of our Lord, Jesus Christ...(but) there shall be false teachers among you, who privily shall bring in damnable heresies... And many shall follow their pernicious ways; by reason of whom the way of truth shall be evil spoken of. And through covetousness shall they with feigned (fabled) words make merchandise of you"**. (II Peter 1:16, 2:1-3)

One may pray the Prayer of Jabez 'til he is blue in the face. One may purchase all of the various "Jabez" merchandise; the books, the calendars, the Jabez stones, the t-shirts, etc. etc. And all that will happen as a result is that someone will have made "merchandise of you".

"Lay not up for yourselves treasures upon earth, where moth and rust doth corrupt, and where thieves break through and steal: but lay up for yourselves treasures in heaven...for where your treasure is, there shall your heart be also."

(Matthew 6:19-21)

6

Living *on* Little For God

"How will we ever pay this month's bills"? I balanced the dollars in our account against the stack of bills on the floor in front of me, and knew that we were in serious trouble. Our carpet cleaning business was barely keeping us afloat, and in the winter months work was even more scarce. But by the grace of God and the sweat of hard work we had always pulled through.

"I'll just have to make more calls, offer lower prices, and work longer hours", I thought to myself. I offered our troubles to the Lord in prayer as so many times before, and then got up to go to work.

When the telephone rang my first thought was, "Wow, that was quick". Was it was one of my customers calling? Maybe one of the hotels I cleaned carpet for needed some emergency work right away. Or maybe it was Publisher's Clearing House calling to inform me that I had just won a million dollars! Yeah right. Even a small upholstery cleaning job would help at this point.

I answered the phone with great expectation. And although it was good to hear the voice of my wife, Sandra, on the other end, I was a little bit disappointed that my prayer had not been answered instantaneously. She was calling from a pay phone, and I could hear the voice of a child crying in the background.

"Where are you", I asked, "Is everything O.K.?

Sandra explained how she had been at home earlier when she got a call from a teenage girl in trouble. Immediately she had dropped what she was doing, packed the kids up in the car, and headed off into the unknown to help someone she had never met.

"She told me that you had talked to her as she was headed into an abortion clinic in Austin three months ago", Sandra explained, "and that you gave her a piece of paper with your phone number on it. She said that you had offered her help and a place to stay".

I remembered the girl immediately. Her name was Monique. She was eighteen or nineteen years old, three months pregnant, and had a one year old daughter. I remember the day I met her on the sidewalk in front of an abortion clinic in Austin, Texas.

It was cold that day, and I could tell from the expression on her face that she was scared and hurting. The baby she carried in her womb was now in the second trimester of his life, and the abortionist refused to do the "job" for the amount of cash she had on her.

I remembered the desperate look on her face as she left the clinic. And I remembered having given her our phone number and a little note saying that we would help her any way we could.

When Sandra found her that day Monique was six months pregnant and sitting next to her daughter with a couple of plastic garbage sacks filled with their clothes. She said that she had been kicked out of her boyfriend's apartment. She was homeless, helpless, and had no money.

"I'll get a room ready... bring her home, God will make a way", I said over the phone, not sure of anything except for the fact that we were in the center of God's will.

My will in the flesh would have been to say, "No, we can't.... we're completely buried in bills... we must think of our own family first... When God blesses us a little more, then we will begin to bless others". Or I could have said, "We'll have to pray about it first", putting the blame on God for my lack of love and will to sacrifice for the cause of Christ. Or I could have simply told Sandra to take her to the Salvation Army or some government funded shelter.

But I had seen God's miraculous provision before many times. And I knew that His Word was true, "Cast thy burden upon the Lord, and He shall sustain thee".

Little did we know at the time, that the Lord was not only giving us an opportunity to suffer, or at least be inconvenienced for Christ's sake, but He was also going to provide an opportunity to others to see if they would help as they saw our sacrifice and great need. Would other believers help us with this burden, or would they "pass by on the other side", as the Levite did to the suffering stranger on the road to Jericho?

One month I remember we had to sell our furniture to pay the rent.

I cried the day a local businessman in Austin gave me a $20 bill to help out with food for the girl and her children. The needs were so great.

When it looked like we would have to sell our car also, a dear friend, Don, a member of the First Baptist Church in Georgetown, gave us his car to sell instead. We traded it to our landlord for three months rent.

A Catholic woman named Flo, who prayed in front of abortion clinics in Austin on a regular basis, gave us gift certificates for groceries many times. And we made it through.

At the time we only had three children. Ryan was five, Rebekah was one, and Emily was due at about the same time as

Monique's baby. So we just moved Ryan and Rebekah into a bedroom together, and made a room available for Monique. We were living in a single wide three bedroom mobile home that rented for $260 a month. (I told Sandra many times that we did not deserve to live in such luxury. With hot and cold running water, air conditioning and heat, we lived better than Pontius Pilate, the governor who condemned Christ to death. And how could we ever forget the place we lived before that… a 1953 one bedroom trailer that had twenty-one dead scorpions under the living room sofa the day we moved in!)

So we were not complaining, it was just a little tough at times. But you know, God never said that obedience to Him would be easy. There is no place in the Bible that says the way of Christ is a cake walk.

I have heard Christians claim that they knew that they were in God's will because everything was "going so smoothly" in their lives. Another claim made by many believers goes something like this… "I knew that it was God's will because everything just fell in place". This type of thinking is not supported in Scripture. In fact, most of the great men and women of Scripture met with adversity on a daily basis in their efforts to do the will of God.

If the Apostle Paul had adopted such reason he would not have continued to travel about preaching the Gospel. As we read in chapter one of this book, "he was jailed, beaten, stoned, shipwrecked, (and) robbed" while doing the will of God. Adversity just comes with the territory. But through it all God was with Paul; leading him, guiding him, comforting him, and providing for his every need.

And so, by the example of Christ and the apostles, we also pressed on. But it was not a time of ease. Neither was it a time of prosperity. I had made a commitment years earlier that we would never accept help from government welfare programs.

This conviction was instilled in me by my mother who gave blood every Thursday to provide milk money for us children.

We believed, and still do, that any needs within the family of God that cannot be met through prayer and hard work, should be met by those of the local church and fellow believers. It is a Biblical principle that is all but lost in our culture. We had been offered "free" milk, cheese, and butter from the WIC program on more than one occasion, but chose to stand on our principles instead.

It was hard. The road was rough. But we did not turn back. And God heard our prayers, and He sustained us. We did not have money for fast food, dining out, and luxury items like new clothes. We bought everything at second hand stores, if we bought anything at all. And we never missed a meal. God be praised.

Then when the time came, Monique went into labor and delivered a son. And she called his name Derek. And we thank God to this day for His wonderful provision during those most trying times.

...of their own substance

In Bruce Wilkinson's multi-million dollar selling book *"The Prayer of Jabez"* the author has a chapter entitled, *"Living Large for God".* In this chapter the author encourages the reader to ask God to *"enlarge (his) territory."*

Wilkinson says, *"When Jabez cried out to God, 'Enlarge my territory,' he was looking at his present circumstances and concluding, 'Surely I was born for more than this!'...everything you've put under my care, O Lord- take it, and enlarge it. If Jabez had worked on Wall Street, he might have prayed, 'Lord, increase the value of my investment portfolios."*

Wilkinson then goes on to sanction such requests from God with an 'ends justifies the means' approach to covetousness. In other words, it is okay to ask God for more things, lands, houses, money, business, investment portfolios, etc. if the intention is to *"influence"* others for God with these things after they have been acquired.

According to Wilkinson, Christians should pray, *"Bless me Lord, and while you're at it … bless me a lot…enlarge my territories."* And then they will automatically receive *"blessings on a scale they hadn't imagined possible."* After these huge blessings arrive they will then see *"God stretch the limits of their influence…."*

"Influence"? Why do we hear so much talk of *"influence"*? Jesus never tried to influence anyone. The Apostles' lives in the book of Acts provide us with zero accounts where they attempted to *"influence"* others for God. Jesus' last command before His ascension was that we **"go into all the world making disciples of all nations, and teaching them to obey all things whatsoever I have commanded you."** This is the Great Commission. Can you imagine the watered down pathetic effect of a commission to "go into the world and influence people"?

The problem with Christianity in America today is not that believers have limited *"resources"*, *"contacts"*, and *"opportunities"* to *"influence"* others for the kingdom of God. The problem is that Christians in America and Europe refuse to use the massive bounty of resources, contacts, and opportunities for ministry God has already given them.

American Christians have grown obese and lazy, eating up the "blessings" from the hand of God and throwing the scraps back into His lap.

Christians in America do not need *"…to ask for more and more again, much more than you ever thought to ask Him for"*, as Wilkinson preaches in his Jabez books. Christians need to use all the wealth, and bounty, and time, and energy, and health **God has already provided**, and serve Him in the world!

The Bible says that "he that is faithful in least (little things) is also faithful in much", but the man that has not used the little that God has given him, will also not be faithful if God gives Him more (Luke 16:10).

In the eighth Chapter of Luke we find several women whom the writer tells us ministered **"of their own substance"** to support Jesus and the disciples as they went from city to city preaching the Good News. These women did not pray the prayer of Jabez. They did not *"ask for more, and more again"* as Wilkinson teaches his followers. They **"ministered of their own substance"**. They used what God had already given them, knowing that He had already provided for their every need. They gave their all. And Christ did not admonish them to do any other.

There is no warehouse in heaven with little white boxes filled with regret for *"blessings God wanted to give… while on earth…"*, but did not give because these women did not ask.

Jesus never reprimanded these women for ministering **"of their own substance"**, instead of *"begging for His blessing"*, as Wilkinson has taught.

"So are you saying that I should never ask God for anything?"

Of course not, the Scriptures declare that you should offer **everything** up to God in prayer.

You are told to make your requests known, and all the while to be ever conscious that, "…**your Father knoweth what things ye have need of before ye ask Him**", as it says in Matthew chapter six. But Christians are also admonished to **"be content with such things as ye have"**, knowing that Jesus has said, **"I will never leave thee, nor forsake thee"**. (Hebrews 13:5)

We must also remember that we were bought with a price, even the blood of the Lord, Jesus Christ, **"Ye are not your own, for ye are bought with a price"**. **Jesus died on the Cross to reconcile us to God.** <u>And so all that we have and are belongs to Him and should be used for His Kingdom and His glory.</u>

It is true that the greatest feats of history concerning the Gospel of Jesus Christ have been accomplished with little. History is filled with stories of Christians accomplishing amazing tasks with little to nothing. God has never forsaken the man, woman, or child who has used the little they have for His glory. I encourage the reader of this book to see themselves as Jesus does, daily ministers of God's love, mercy, and kindness in a fallen world. Seek God for your place in His plan and He will show you how you can use whatever He has given you; arms, legs, eyes, ears, a car, spare change, whatever you have and are for the Gospel of our Lord, Jesus Christ!

In Bruce Wilkinson's *"The Prayer of Jabez"*, chapter three, entitled *"Living large for God"*, the author seems to despise small beginnings and the daily cross bearing that Jesus preached. In keeping with the popular prosperity message of our time, he says on page forty-four, **"When you take little steps, you don't need God."**

This, of course, is not true. Wilkinson is greatly deceived.

We who believe realize our great need for God's leading, guidance, and direction every moment of our earthly pilgrimage. It is the little steps, the daily reliance upon our Lord for both the spiritual and physical sustenance needed to go forward, that has historically advanced the cause of Christ from generation to generation.

On page 33 of Wilkinson's Jabez book for adults he talks about a group of college students who took his advice to *"live large for God"*, and *"ask Him for something big…"*. The students get together and decide to *"take an island for God"*, as Wilkinson had suggested.

After deciding on the island of Trinidad they charter a plane and go in for a *"summer of ministry"*. Trinidad is a fun place to "minister" in the summer. In keeping with Wilkinson's assertion that God wants a life of *"adventure, excitement, and fun"* for his *"most honored servants"*, a summer trip to Trinidad for a large Christian college would be a most pleasant way of "serving the Lord". I am not condemning those who minister at popular summer vacation spots with suitcases void of swimsuits, tanning lotions, and beach combers. I'm sure there must have been those who went for the express purpose of advancing the Gospel of Jesus Christ and only a secondary benefit of sunshine, comfort and enjoyment. But you understand very well why Wilkinson suggested Trinidad over Sudan, Afghanistan, or Nicaragua.

Ministry is not always *"adventure, excitement, and lots of fun"*, as Wilkinson claims on page one of His *"Jabez for Kids"* book. Ministry is not always *"something big... something huge."*

In poverty and great sacrifice the illegal house church movement of China has grown from a few thousand to millions upon millions in the past twenty years. One small step at a time these believers, under incredible persecution, have covered the entire continent with the Good News of the cross of Christ!

No matter what financial situation you may find yourself in today, God has a purpose and a plan of daily ministry for your life. You need not wait on some future date of *"blessing"* before you decide to act. **God has given each of us what He intends for us to use for Him today.**

One has more time, another more money. One has better health, another has more talent. Whatever your lot in this Life, thank God for it! Then go forward this very moment seeking the course of ministry He has chosen you for; rendering all that you are or will ever be, all that you have or will ever have for His Kingdom and His glory, in Jesus' Name!

"I have learned, in whatsoever state I am, therewith to be content. I know both how to be abased and how to abound: everywhere and in all things I am instructed both to be full and to be hungry, both to abound and to suffer need... I can do all things through Christ which strengtheneth me."

(Phillipians 4:12-13)

7
Three Reasons
God will not Hear

The Preface of Bruce Wilkinson's, *"The Prayer of Jabez"* begins:

"Dear Reader,

I want to teach you how to pray a daring prayer that <u>God always</u> <u>answers</u>...the key to a life of extra-ordinary favor with God."

Before the author even begins page one of his book the foundation for grave error has already been laid. *"One sentence... tucked away in the Bible"*, a *"prayer that God <u>always</u> answers"*?

Could it be? Could a twenty-first century author have uncovered a secret prayer "buried" in Scripture for over 2000 years that God <u>always</u> answers?

Did God choose a Georgia millionaire named Bruce Wilkinson to reveal the secrets of an Old Testament prayer hidden from generations past?

How could the greatest theologians and martyrs of the past two millennia have missed this *"one sentence"* of Scripture that brings about such an awesome *"transformation"*?

Jesus Himself never mentioned a word about the *"miracle of Jabez"*, as Wilkinson calls it, yet the author claims the Jabez prayer *"contains the key to a life of extra-ordinary favor with God"*?

Certainly Jesus would have said something about this to the

great crowds that gathered to hear Him speak. Certainly if there was something to this *"Jabez revolution"*, Jesus would have at least alluded to it at some point in His earthly ministry.

When the disciples came to Christ saying, "Teach us to pray", would He have intentionally withheld from them *"the key to a life of extra-ordinary favor with God"*?

Again, I must reiterate that the Bible warns us in the last days **"there shall be false teachers among you"** who would bring in damnable heresies, and that many would be deceived.

With all the earnestness I have I tell you, do not be deceived. There is no new revelation in Scripture. Searching for secret and hidden things in Gods Word is the driving force behind all pseudo-Christian cults in the world today.

Allow me to publish this truth once more:

The prayer of a repentant sinner calling on the Name of Jesus Christ for salvation is the only prayer that *"God always answers"*.

No teacher, no pastor, no theologian, no priest, no millionaire author on earth can find or invent any prayer that God is bound or obligated to answer or hear. In fact, God has revealed to all generations past through His word that the prayers of many go unanswered.

What? God is not obligated to answer my prayer?

Absolutely not.

"Then shall they call upon me, but I will not answer.." (Proverbs 1:28)

"Not answer", you say in stunned disbelief, "Why would God

not answer?".

The text in Proverbs Chapter one goes on to answer that question. They hated knowledge, they did not choose to fear the Lord, they would not receive the counsel of God, and they despised all of His reproof. **"Therefore shall they eat of the fruit of their own way."** (Proverbs 1:31)

All of the reasons stated above; the hating of knowledge, the choice not to fear God, and the refusal to accept godly counsel and reproof are all signs of a hard and impenitent heart. This passage of Scripture describes those who are set in their ways. They are headstrong, proud, and haughty. They hate knowledge. They despise the knowledge and wisdom that comes from consuming the Word of God. They choose not to fear God, even though the Bible says "the fear of God is the beginning of wisdom". They refuse the counsel of godly men and women who seek to help them. Then finally they despise all of God's reproof.

Going forward in their rebellion, in an unapproachable spirit of arrogance and self- assuredness they fall into a situation of calamity. And God says He will not answer their prayers when they call on him, "...**I will not answer**... therefore shall they eat of the fruit of their own way".

I see many today in this generation who in times of great trouble and distress call upon God to help them. But they do not call to God from a humble heart that seeks repentance and forgiveness. **They seek the help of God to get them out of their present crises with no intention whatsoever of being faithful to God after he has rescued them.**

My associate pastor at Burnet Bible Church, Chris Keys, has been imprisoned in many of the major jail systems across America. He has been behind bars for the cause of Christ in Los Angeles, Atlanta, and many other large cities, sometimes for nothing more than praying on a public sidewalk in front of an abortion clinic.

Many times a fellow prisoner, knowing Chris to be a pastor and a just man, has asked him to pray for an upcoming court appearance. However, I have heard him tell how the vast majority of those seeking prayer while in jail only seek to save their own skin.

When Chris asks them if they are willing to pray that God's will is done, even if it means spending twenty years in prison for their crimes, the answer is usually "No".

In the same way many today pray for Divine protection and assistance, and yet are not willing to leave their sins behind, or pay the earthly penalties associated with those sins. Many continue in a life of rebellion against God and yet expect Him to rescue them in times of trouble and distress, just because they call on Him.

But God is not obligated to answer the prayers of unrepentant and defiant sinners who are seeking nothing more than self-preservation. **Jesus said, "For whosoever will save his life shall lose it: and whosoever will lose his life for my sake shall find it."** (Matthew 16:25)

The words of Bob Dylan from his album entitled "Saved" address this human inclination well...

"Do you ever wonder, just what God requires? You think He's just an errand boy to satisfy your wandering desires... When you gonna wake-up... and strengthen the things that remain?"

Reason number one that God will not hear:

"If I regard iniquity in my heart the Lord will not hear me." (Psalm 66:18)

How many times do believers go before God in prayer while harboring some secret sin in their lives? How often do professing believers in churches across our land expect an answer from God in the midst of open rebellion?

If this is your present situation I must ask you the question, "Why go to God with your requests at all? If you are showing some regard for a certain sin in your life, why present your petitions to ears that have become weary of your hard-heartedness? Why pray at all if you know that the Lord is not going to hear you"?

You may go to God confessing your sins and seeking forgiveness and cleansing. You may pour out your heart to God in humility asking Him for grace in your hour of temptation. You may cry out to God, "Be merciful to me a sinner" seeking strength in the Spirit against the daily trappings of the adversary. But do not go before God regarding or harboring some secret sin in your life, and think that He will hear from heaven. If you regard or justify some sin in your life understand that your prayer life will be powerless, and you will only be "spinning your wheels".

Melissa was eight years old when she responded to the message of the Gospel. The evangelist who spoke that Sunday morning at her church was speaking on the topic of prayer. "The only prayer that God always answers", he preached, "is a prayer of repentance and faith in the finished work of Jesus Christ on the Cross to forgive our sins." Melissa prayed with her mother, and put her trust in the Lord that day.

Her parents home-schooled her until she turned fourteen. But peer pressure from her public educated friends caused Melissa to turn against the counsel, guidance, and authority of her parents. One day, seemingly out of the blue, Melissa demanded that her parents allow her to go to the local public school so that she could "have some fun" like all of her friends and "have a normal childhood".

After days of arguing and bickering Melissa's parents finally gave in and enrolled her at the local public high school.

Within weeks Melissa began to press her parents to buy "some normal clothes" for her. Her immodesty increased almost daily until one day Melissa's parents did not recognize her as she walked past them on a public sidewalk.

Next came the boyfriends. Melissa's parents had always taught their daughter that dating was not a custom of Christianity. They had always told her growing up that she would one day be "courted", and that for the purpose of seeking a godly husband, not just to "have some fun". But Melissa had been taught by her worldly peers that "you only go around once" so "you better get all you can when you can".

She had seen the world, loved what she saw, and left Christ far behind. She listened to music that glorified sex and friendship with the world. She went to movies with her friends where they enjoyed the continual breaking of the ten commandments on the "silver screen". She lived in a world of sensuality and rebellion against authority.

Many times the still small voice of God in her conscience called her to repentance, but she would not give in.

Then one day, without warning, her entire life seemed to just fall apart. The boyfriend she had hoped to marry left her for someone a little younger and a little prettier. She lost her job. The motor in her car seized up. Two weeks later she realized that she was pregnant with the child of a man that did not love her or her baby.

Melissa was angry with God. She had never stopped praying. She had prayed daily, in fact. She had prayed for good health.

She had prayed for God's blessings on her life. She had prayed for raises at work. She even prayed for her family and friends. But all the while she was living in rebellion against God, and now she was reaping the fruit of her own way. Melissa became bitter, angry, and resentful. All her prayers were going unanswered. It was as if, she thought, **God was not even listening.**

Melissa's parents had prayed on their knees into the night for their daughter on many occasions. They prayed that God would draw her back to Him and restore her to them. But their prayers, too, seemed to go unanswered.

Then one day, after crying out to God for an hour, Melissa's father stumbled upon a very distressing and seemingly harsh word of Scripture in the book of Proverbs in the Bible.

"Then shall they call upon me, but I will not answer…" (Proverbs 1:28)

"Not answer?", her father thought to himself, "Why would God not answer someone who is calling upon him?"

But as he read further he understood:

"For they hated knowledge, and did not choose the fear of the Lord; They would (have) none of my counsel; they despised My reproof… therefore shall they eat of the fruit of their own way".

Melissa's father fell to his knees in deep sorrow. He knew now that he was partially to blame for the course of his daughter. He had not feared the Lord. He had not received God's counsel to turn from lustful thoughts and unholy practices as Melissa was growing up. **He had given in a thousand times to impure thoughts and set his heart to meditate on the vulgar images streaming forth from his television.** God had reproved him time and again, but he had always returned to wallowing in the mire. He knew that Jesus said that to look upon a woman with lust is adultery of the heart, but he had always found some way to justify it in his mind.

Melissa's mother was instantly convicted, too. She now saw that her rebellion in the home against her husband's authority had transferred to her daughter. **She cried tears of repentance as she realized that her insubmissive behavior during Melissa's childhood had schooled her daughter in the art of rebellion.** She knew that God's Word said that she was to reverence her husband and 'submit' to him as unto the Lord, but she had always convinced herself that her rebellion was justified for one reason or another.

"We are now eating of the fruit of our own way", they thought, "and God has not answered our hypocritical prayers". It was on that day that Melissa's parents realized what the Psalmist had meant three thousand years ago when he said, "If I regard iniquity in my heart, the Lord will not hear me".

All of the instances of their rebellion were now before their faces. All of the skeletons in their closet stood before them, and they despised what they had once loved. All of their sins; the lust, the rebellion, the insubmission, were now being identified and exposed like criminals in a police line-up. And as they dealt with each one of these sins before God a weight was lifted, a cloud evaporated, and God's plan and purpose in it all seemed to shine down from heaven with a new and blinding light.

Melissa was stunned the day her parents showed up at her apartment. As her parents sat on her sofa confessing their hypocrisy over the years Melissa began to cry. She now understood for the first time in her life what Jesus meant when He said, **"As many as I love, I rebuke, and chasten..."** Together they cried tears of joy, as a family that had received a child back from the dead. They confessed their sins and faults to one another, and prayed for forgiveness and healing.

Melissa and her baby moved back home with her parents. Life is not easy, but with the dawning of each new day they sense the *favor* of God on their lives. How longsuffering is the Lord with those whom He loves. As the Scriptures declare, **"His mercy endureth forever"**. Now they are witnesses of His enduring mercy. Now they are witnesses of His infinite love. And the "peace that passeth understanding" floods their lives as they make their requests known to the One who answers prayers.

<u>Reason number two that God will not hear:</u>

"Ye ask and receive not, because ye ask amiss, that ye may consume it upon your lusts."

(James 4:3)

I was heart broken as I read the seemingly deliberate perversion of the teaching of the Apostle James concerning prayer by the author of *"The Prayer of Jabez"*.

On page 27 of his book, Bruce Wilkinson quotes St. James as saying *"You do not have, because you do not ask"*.

Like Oral Roberts, who claimed that God would strike him dead if he did not raise eight million dollars for his "ministry", and like Benny Hinn, the televangelist who claims to have healed more people than Jesus and the Apostles put together, **Wilkinson takes this same verse of Scripture completely out of context** to support his blatant heresy.

Every money-grubbing, prosperity preaching, false prophet of the past forty years has used this same verse to promote his or her doctrine. And they all have one thing in common... They all get filthy rich selling these false teachings to the undiscerning.

The following verse of Scripture is what the Apostle actually said in Chapter four of the book of James with Wilkinson's "out of context" quote in italics.

"Ye lust, and have not: ye kill and desire to have, and cannot obtain: ye fight and war, yet *ye have not, because ye ask not.* Ye ask, and receive not, because ye ask amiss, that ye may consume it upon your lusts. Ye adulterers and adulteresses, know ye not that friendship with the world is enmity with God? Whosoever therefore shall be a friend of the world is the enemy of God." (James 4: 2-4)

Did Wilkinson think that no one would reference the verse he claimed to quote? Too many times believers fail to check out teachings with the Bible and so are led astray.

James was dealing with the broad range of covetous behaviors. He taught us in verse one that "lusts" war in our members; that is the members of our flesh. A man lusts or covets for something and cannot get it. Some allow their lust for what others have to drive them to kill to get what they want. Some fight and war to get what they want and cannot obtain. A man does not have because he does not ask, and then when he asks he does not receive because he asks "amiss" (or with the wrong motives), for the purpose of gratifying the desires of his flesh.

James attacked the basic nature of the carnal man, and then identifies the desires craved by the flesh as friendship with the world, which makes a man the enemy of God.

As I said in Chapter Six, it is not that we need *"more from God"*, as Wilkinson preaches, it is that we have not used for His glory the resources, time, money, and contacts in the world that He has already provided.

This, of course, is not all-inclusive. I have witnessed many Christians whose prayer life is powerful; who assign all that

God gives them to be used in some way for His Kingdom. **But the vast majority of professing believers in our world today view luxury as necessity, and so never seem to have quite enough to serve God on a daily basis.**

<u>Reason Number Three that God Will Not Hear:</u>

"And when ye spread forth your hands, I will hide mine eyes from you: yea, when ye make many prayers, <u>I will not hear</u>: your hands are full of blood."

(Isaiah 1: 15)

The place was Germany, the year 1941. Hitler's secret police, the "Gestapo", raided the homes of Jews, confiscating their property and separating their family members from one another.

All across the nation of Germany communities watched as their Jewish neighbors were hustled away at gunpoint in the middle of the night and in broad daylight.

Fathers were sent to forced labor and concentration camps where they were worked to death, their corpses incinerated in large ovens. Older women and mothers were sent to similar camps to work until they were no longer of any profit. Young girls and teenagers were sent to special camps to become the sex slaves of German soldiers. Pregnant girls and infants were sent to laboratories for medical experimentation. "Useless eaters", the handicapped, and the elderly were sent to the "showers", stripped naked of all their earthly possessions, only to find that these showers were really gas chambers where they would breath their last.

And German society went on as usual.

Businesses continued to sell their products…

Banks continued to loan their money…

And churches continued to hold their services on Sunday.

An elderly woman was interviewed years ago about her youthful days growing up in the late 1930's in a small German town. She told how a railroad ran directly behind the church her family attended in the country. On many Sunday mornings, while the congregation sang praises to Jesus, they could hear the voices of Jewish men, women and children on cattle cars screaming for help as the trains passed by the church on their way to the death camps.

"What did you do?", asked a member of the media who was interviewing her.

"We just sang louder" was her response.

Deaf to the cries of those being led away to the slaughter, these "Christians" did nothing to stop the butchery of their neighbors.

"But it was the law", one minister of a Dutch reformed church said in defense, "We were only obeying the law… to house a Jew or care for one of their orphaned babies would have been against the law, and Christians must obey the law."

In order to protect their earthly possessions, positions, and affluence most professing Christians conveniently looked the other way even though they knew that innocent human beings were being "eliminated" in their own neighborhoods.
Recently it was asked why the church in Germany did not rise up and put an end to the slaughter. "Why didn't the church

stand up and help them?", someone asked.

Another standing by answered, **"The church did stand up...**
only when it stood up, it just wasn't that big".

The Ten Boom family of Holland hid Jews in a secret room in
their house after the Nazi occupation of World War II. When
the pastor of a local church condemned him and his sons and
daughters for taking in a Jewish baby "against the law" eighty
six year old "Papa Ten Boom" looked at his daughters and said,
"Just because a mouse lives in a cookie jar, doesn't necessarily
make him a cookie".

Just because there were church buildings on every street corner
in Germany does not necessarily mean that those buildings
were full of Christians.

In 1973 the United States Supreme Court overturned the laws
of all fifty states protecting unborn children from death by
abortion. Since that date nearly 50 million pre-born infants
have been "legally" put to death at American abortion facilities.

I have video taped footage of Los Angeles police beating
Christians with their batons. The victims were both young and
old, men and women. Their crime? ...praying on their knees on
the public sidewalk in front of an abortion clinic. Hundreds of
believers from every denomination of Christianity poured into
the streets in an effort to save innocent children from being
violently ripped from their mother's wombs.

But the "authorities" of the City of Los Angeles ordered the
Christians to leave the streets. Dozens of believers were on their
faces praying. Others sat and prayed. Some stood in front of the
clinic doors hoping to prevent the abortionist from entering.
After all, if he could not get inside, then he could not kill.
Police officers poured into the area like a river. In full riot gear,
on horseback, and on foot they moved against the Christians

striking blows from their batons and spraying mace. A Baptist youth pastor, who is kneeling and praying, is dragged away by police officers using "pain compliance" tortures. He is later dismissed from employment by the senior pastor for his persistent acts of mercy.

A Catholic priest is dragged by his clerical collar by several officers of the LAPD; his face red from being choked, his knees limply raking across the pavement. A young Christian man is raised from his knees by police with nunchukas, his arms bent backwards above his head. In the video, his forearm is seen to snap in two, breaking completely in half.

Other Christians who are on their knees praying are continually vaulted in the rib cage with police night sticks and dragged off to jail.

In excess of 75 thousand arrests were made in America in less than 10 years as a remnant of the church stood up peacefully against the slaughter of innocent children. But the church at large in America refused to leave their air conditioned houses of worship to save a few of their little neighbors from being slain.

Like the handful of German Christians in Nazi Germany in the 1930's and 1940's who hid Jews from the Gestapo, this faithful remnant in America has suffered persecution and imprisonment, the loss of homes and jobs, as they lay down their lives to save a few of the 4400 pre-born children who are being brutally slaughtered each and every day.

Many churches in America have never even so much as lifted a prayer to God on behalf of the unborn. In fact, most of the churches in America, like the "patriotic" churches of Germany during that holocaust, have vocally and publicly reprimanded their brothers and sisters who laid down their lives to defend those who could not defend themselves.

As the voices of the blood of nearly 50 million unborn children murdered in America since 1973 rise up to God in heaven, the vast majority of our churches have remained silent.

Like the church in Germany with the railroad running directly behind it, the Christians of our nation ignore the cries of those being led away to slaughter. They do not pray for the unborn. They do not seek to save those which are being lost to the abortionists knife...

They just sing louder.

They know that the blood of innocent children is being shed, and choose to do nothing to intervene on the behalf of those whose lives are being taken from them with great violence.

They conveniently forget that God says in His Word that we are to **"deliver those being drawn unto death, and them that are ready to be slain."** (Proverbs 24:11)

We have the greatest "worship and praise" services ever constructed in the history of the world, yet all the while the voices of those being led away to slaughter go unheeded.

The voices of the unborn are painfully loud and haunting in the hearing of those who have a heart for the things of God. But for those who live "as unto themselves" the cries of the babies are but a faint whisper that can easily be overcome by the voices of jubilant praise.

Our churches are convinced that God in heaven is pleased with this kind of praise and worship. And so each Sunday morning after the worship leaders have brought their congregation to "a new level" of emotion, the masses flow from their churches to the restaurants for yet another round of feasting on the delicacies of our time.

And all the while the babies cry for help.

Sing louder... completely disregard the voice of their terror... in the face of their bitter and mournful cry... "Help us, please help us!"....just sing louder.

And to bring the full chastening of God down upon this wicked self-serving church, in an age when rivers of blood are flowing in the streets, add to it all the words... *"Bless me, Lord, Bless me indeed... enlarge my borders..."!*

Not only have we refused to stop the slaughter taking place outside of our church walls, we have also participated in the bloodshed of children within the walls of our churches. Our so-called houses of prayer and worship and praise are filled with the bloodshed of abortion. Christian mothers have driven their own daughters to abortion clinics to pay a man to murder their grandbabies. Pastors and deacons have counseled teenage girls to sacrifice their own children on the altar of convenience and economics.

And we expect our prayers to be heard.

"...I will not hear... your hands are full of blood."
(Isaiah 1:15)

The church in America must repent of these atrocities. We must repent of our crimes and sins of omission; not helping those who are being dragged away to slaughter, and those of commission; participating as accessories to the murder of pre-born infants.

If our prayers are ever to be heard by God, in the Name of Jesus Christ, we must repent.

"Take thou away from me the noise of thy songs; for I will not hear the melody of thy viols...

And I will turn your feasts into mourning, and all your songs into lamentation...

I will not turn away the punishment thereof; because they have ripped up the woman with child ... that they might enlarge their borders..."

(From the book of Amos in the Bible)

8
Divine Appointments

At four o'clock in the morning I climbed into bed. I had just finished the sermon for the funeral of a six-week old baby, and was physically, emotionally, and spiritually exhausted. After a few restless hours of sleep Sandra awakened me, and I rolled out of bed and darted to the shower.

It was my second funeral in less than a week. A few days earlier my grandmother had died. She suffered a huge heart attack the day after communion Sunday. I was thankful that God allowed me to be with her for an hour before she was Star Flighted to an Austin hospital. But little did I know that when the side door of the helicopter closed between us I would never see her alive again. At her funeral there were songs of sorrow interspersed with songs of joy. She had lived a long and good life. She loved the Lord, and was ready to meet Him.

But the funeral of little Adrian was crushing. His parents were in their teens and he was their first-born. Only three weeks earlier the parents had brought him to church to be dedicated to the Lord. Now they were heart-broken, sitting in front of that little blue casket, leaning over in the arms of close relatives moaning and weeping. It was tragic.

Songs were sung that could not revive the hearts of those who were mourning. Words were spoken that could not cure a sorrow that time alone could begin to heal. And as the clouds rolled by overhead the mourners dispersed, one by one, and two by two.

My next stop was the local nursing home for a quick visit and then I was off to work. (I have not taken a salary at Burnet Bible

Church during my five years as pastor, and so have operated a business part-time to pay the bills).

It was a hot summer day. My work was outdoors, and by 5 p.m. I was a walking zombie.

I now had about an hour to drive somewhere, get a bite to eat, and be back at my place of business in time for a 6 p.m. appointment. If all went as planned I would be finished at work, and back home by about 10 p.m. in time to see my wife's beautiful face before bedtime.

In the parking lot of Luby's cafeteria I hung my head down and cried out to the Lord, "Father, I need help... I'm exhausted... I can't take anymore... I'm completely spent... Lord.. there's only so much a man can bear."

But when I lifted my head, my eyes fell on a man coming across the parking lot of the cafeteria. He was dressed in ragged blue jeans and a dirty t-shirt. His right arm and leg were deformed and a severe limp caused him to drag the one leg as he walked.

"God forgive me," I whispered to the Lord, "Forgive me for complaining when I have been given so much". I met him crossing the parking lot and introduced myself. He said his name was Ray, and he asked me if I could drive him another mile to his home. I hesitated, briefly considering my own petty problems, and then said, "Sure, but first let me buy you dinner". Ray was elated, and I was most grateful that God's plan included food for both of us!

We got our trays, filled them with food, and then went to wash up. I washed my hands, and Ray washed his hand, and we sat down to pray. I asked the blessing, prayed for my new friend, and then we both dug in for a wonderful meal.

While we ate Ray told me his life's story.

When he was six years old he was hit by an eighteen wheeler semi-truck while crossing the street. His right arm and leg were severely crushed. After getting out of the hospital his parents decided to give him away to a government institution that could better deal with his "situation".

On the outside I was smiling and choking down my food, but on the inside I was crying like a baby.

"How could a mother and father give away their own sweet baby boy", I thought, "What kind of inhuman heartless monsters would abandon their own six year old child because he was handicapped?"

Ray's story got worse. He was placed in one "home" after another. In one "home" he was sexually abused by a pastor and his wife. Now he was working at a car wash drying off vehicles with his one good hand and living in a government home for handicapped men.

I asked Ray if he attended church in Austin. He told me that a man picked him up and took him to a church on Sundays.

On our drive back to Ray's house he said, "I know a Christian song, too."

"Really," I said, "Which one?" He went on to sing an entire verse and chorus to "Jesus loves me, this I know." As I let Ray off we shook hands and made a deal to remember to pray for each other.

On my drive to my business appointment a verse of Scripture came to mind. It is from the book of Luke and it is Jesus speaking. I don't think anyone will ever sell a popular book based on this little verse *"tucked away in the Bible."* I don't think anyone will ever get rich selling little stones, calendars, or wall plaques with this verse on it. But maybe, just maybe a few people will take it to heart, and be blessed. And Jesus will smile…

"When thou makest a dinner or a supper, call not thy friends, nor thy brethren, neither thy kinsmen, nor thy rich neighbors; lest they also bid thee again, and a recompence (payment) be made thee.

But when thou makest a feast, call the poor, the maimed, the lame, the blind: <u>And thou shalt be blessed</u>; for they cannot recompence (repay) thee: for thou shalt be recompensed at the resurrection of the just."

As a young man in my twenties I remember sitting in my car in the parking lot of a Christian bookstore. It was a nice day and I had the window's rolled down when a teenage boy came up and introduced himself, "Is your name Steve?", he asked.

I was in a fairly well known Christian music group at the time that had sold about 30,000 copies of our first LP.

"I'm in a band", he said, "and I just want you to know that I can't wait until I am able to play in front of lots of people and be a witness for Christ".

He seemed to be sincere, but I saw in him a reflection of myself only a short time ago. I had once basked in the "glory" of the Christian music scene. I saw the stars in his eyes, and knew much of the fantasy he was pursuing.

But now I was in a place in my walk with the Lord where I was beginning to see the hypocrisy and carnality of my so-called "music ministry".

I knew now that I had been deceived, believing that I had to look and act like the world in order to reach the world. I had also come to realize that my desire to be seen and heard was a competing passion in my life with that of taking Christ to the lost.

So, I pointed to the parking lot of the strip center behind us and said, "You want to tell others about Jesus? Why wait, Jesus said, 'the fields are ripe unto the harvest'."

I encouraged him to look at the call of Christ on a moment by moment level rather than futuristic. I explained that if he genuinely wanted to be a witness for Christ and the Gospel, he could begin right now.

"Go witness", I said, "There's a whole parking lot full of people who need to hear about Jesus".

His countenance fell. He was no longer eager to "be a witness for Christ." This was not in his plans. He looked for an opportunity to share in the supposed "glory" of Christ, but was not willing to share in His sufferings, or even a little inconvenience.

His perception of "ministry" was flawed, "When I am a successful singer or musician then I will reach others for Jesus". Or, as so many have convinced themselves, "If God gives me money some day, then I'll go and do such and such for him." But, God doesn't work on our terms. He doesn't want us "someday"... God wants us to-day.

God can and will use you this very day for His glory if you will only surrender. No matter if you consider yourself rich or poor, or somewhere in between, the Lord has a moment by moment plan for your life. When Jesus said, "Take up thy cross daily, and follow me", he was charting a course of daily ministry that is applicable to every Christian who has ever lived or will live.

Someone who has a natural talent for singing or playing an instrument can use that gift from God for His glory any time they choose. The problem is that so many "choose" not to sing or play their instrument unless it brings them applause, personal recognition, fame, or fortune.

I thank God that my "claim to fame" was brief and trivial as my heart was not right before God concerning my over-rated "talent" and ministry "potential". When God caused my group's second LP project to collapse, He was blessing me greatly, sparing me a life of sorrow, and pruning me back for the higher calling of a husband and a father.

I then came to the point where I despised my "abilities", and my "talents", and gave them up to God. I told God that I would not use them again until and unless I was sure He wanted me to.

Within a couple of years I was playing music again on a regular basis sensing the pleasure of the Lord. Every Wednesday I played hymns and sang at the local nursing home with another singer from our church. Sandra and the kids visited the "grandmas and grandpas", giving out hugs and smiles and crayon colored pictures, as we sang.

I'll always remember the example of two teenage brothers I knew in high school. They were both mentally handicapped and worked in the fields driving tractors and harvesting lettuce. Johnny and David were hard workers and were known for their strength. It was said that each of the boys could do the work of two full grown men. Neither of the boys was a good speaker. They spoke slowly and with a heavy drawl.

But they loved the Lord, and with the money they earned from working on the local farms they bought Gospel tracts. They would put them out everywhere they went. You may have seen a Gospel tract in a public restroom or at a phone booth in the past. It may have been put there by Johnny or David. The pastor of their church said that he had received calls from people who had come to the Lord as a result of reading those tracts.

You see, many believers today have been deceived into thinking that they must have some special talent or be a part of some special group to have ministry opportunities. Yet Christ and the apostles gave us an example of the Christian life that is in direct contrast. They endeavored to reach everyone with whom they came in contact.

They did not wait for *"divine appointments"* **or** *"Jabez appointments,"* **as Bruce Wilkinson calls them. They knew that every contact in this world was a** *"divine appointment"*, **providing an opportunity to share the Good News with others.** In the flesh they were men of weakness and deficiency. But yielding unreservedly to Jesus, the power of the Holy Spirit worked in them and through them to the glory of God.

They cared for orphans and widows. They fed the hungry. They clothed the naked. They preached Jesus in season and out, when it was convenient and when it was not, whether they were received or hated. In times of poverty; in times of lack, in times of hunger and thirst, "in sleeplessness often", as the Scriptures also declare. They went everywhere preaching the Good News and the whole world was turned upside down for Christ.

"And He said unto me, 'My grace is sufficient for thee: for My strength is made perfect in weakness.' Most gladly therefore will I rather glory in my infirmities, that the power of Christ may rest upon me. Therefore I take pleasure in infirmities, in reproaches, in necessities, in persecutions, in distresses for Christ's sake: for when I am weak, then am I strong."

(2 Corinthians 12:9-10)

9
Jabez means *Pain*

The last Chapter of the book, "*The Prayer of Jabez*", by Bruce Wilkinson is entitled, *"Making Jabez Mine".*

In all of my research of popular Christian books I have found no other author who so intimately embraced a person outside of the Godhead.

Can you imagine a Christian author encouraging you to "Make Moses yours", or "Make Peter yours"? Why would a Christian author promote a personal relationship with an Old Testament figure?

One might understand why the last chapter of the best selling Christian book in years might be entitled, "Making Jesus Mine", but professing and encouraging intimacy with a man who died several hundred years before Christ is more than just a little strange. It is indisputably outside of the realm of Biblical and historical Christian experience. Yet few Christian leaders in the modern era seem to question the direction of this author.

Just because an author sells 65 million dollars worth of books does not mean that he is necessarily doctrinally sound. In fact, one should question the theological purity of any teaching that is accepted by large numbers of various and opposing religions.

I want you to know that I shuddered as I read the final pages of "The Prayer of Jabez" and realized the incredible depth of this worldwide deception.

On the last page of the Bible we find it written, "I, Jesus, have sent mine angel to testify unto you these things in the churches… If any man shall add unto these things, God shall add unto him the plagues that are written in this book: And if any man shall take away from the words of the book of this prophecy, God shall take away his part out of the book of life, and out of the holy city, and from the things which are written in this book".

On page 89 of Wilkinson's book the author suggests that his success is *"evidence of what God's grace AND JABEZ PRAYING CAN DO"*. The inference here is that Christians need more than God's grace for them to be successful in their ministries. In addition one must also engage in *"Jabez praying"*. **This is a clear example of adding to the word of God.** Remember it was Christ who, speaking to the Apostle Paul in the Book of Acts, said, "My grace is sufficient".

Wilkinson continues to add to the Scriptures on the very next page (page 90) when he insists that God answers the prayers of *'those who have a loyal heart AND PRAY THE JABEZ PRAYER"*.

Since when does a Christian have to have a loyal heart *"…AND pray the Jabez prayer"* to get an answer from God?

The error continues on page 91: *"When the merest ray of faith shines in your spirit, the warmth of God's truth infuses you, and you instinctively want to cry out, Oh Lord, please bless… Me! Your spiritual expectations undergo a radical shift…you sense in the deepest recesses of your being the rightness of praying like this… YOU KNOW BEYOND A DOUBT THAT YOU WERE REDEEMED FOR THIS…"*.

Dear God, how could this author ask believers to accept the lie that they were *redeemed for this*? Lord, please open the eyes of your children who have been blinded by the hypnotic and demonic deceptions of this teaching, in Jesus Name!

We who believe "have redemption (are redeemed) through

His blood... reconciled in the body of His flesh through death, (for this purpose) to present you holy and unblameable and unreproveable in His sight..." (Colossians, Chapter 1).

We were not redeemed for the purpose of praying the Jabez prayer, increasing our spiritual expectations, or crying out for more from God. We were redeemed for His glory that we might be presented to Christ, "...holy and unblameable and unreproveable in His sight... a glorious church, not having spot, or wrinkle, or any such thing: but that it should be holy and without blemish."

This brings me to a very important point that every person who has read the Jabez books should not miss. If the reader does not get anything else out of this book, he should make it a point to understand what I am about to say:

Jabez did not have the revelation of Jesus Christ. Though we can assume he looked forward to the coming of "Messiah", as all of the honorable men and women of old, he did not understand the message of the Cross. Jabez did not know that Christ would be born in a stable to a poor family. Jabez did not know that He would come lowly and riding on a donkey. Jabez did not know that the Messiah would suffer and die for the sins of the world. And Jabez was under the law, not grace.

Jabez did not have the light of "...the mystery which hath been hid from ages and from generations" which is now made known to his saints, "which is Christ in you, the hope of glory". Are we so foolish? Having begun in the Spirit, will we be perfected by the flesh (under the law)? (Galatians 3:3)

My second point is this:

The Old Testament should always be interpreted in the light of the New Testament. Without the light of the New Testament shining upon the Old one may lose his way rather quickly. I have seen the faith of countless individual Christians ruined for years by adopting old Testament Jewish traditions and rituals.

The Prayer of David

I can just see the next Christian best-seller to hit the stores. Another Old Testament figure, another Old Testament prayer… and why not, one may argue… if it's in the Bible, why not jump on the next Old Testament prayer bandwagon?

There it is, in every bookstore, every Walmart, every news stand… "The Prayer of David". Hey, David is recorded in the Scriptures as being "a man after God's own heart", right? And after all, we know a great deal more about David than we do about old Jabez.

God answered David's prayer when he went to fight the Philistine giant. God blessed David with wealth and health and children. God's hand was with David in his many battles. God delivered David from the evil intentions of Saul who was seeking to kill him.

Why not *"make a commitment to pray this prayer"* from Psalm, chapter 69 for the next *"thirty days"*:

"Pour out Thine indignation upon them, and let Thy wrathful anger take hold of them. Let their habitation be desolate, and let none dwell in their tents… Let them be blotted out of the book of the living, and not be written with the righteous."

"Little prayer…Big prize".

This is one of David's imprecatory prayers that he prayed against his enemies. David was being pursued. He had been betrayed by a friend. His enemies had made war against him and sought to destroy him. In other places he prayed that his enemies would be childless, their wives widows, and their children faltherless.

The point I am making is this – Just because a prayer is recorded in Scripture does not mean that God intends for all people everywhere at all times to pray it.

Should every Christian in the world be challenged to pray the Prayer of David word for word for thirty days in a row, or as Wilkinson claims he has done with the Jabez prayer, "...*for thirty years"*? I think not.

The teachings of Jesus in the New Testament sheds great light upon these passages. While one might pray for victory in war against the enemies of his or her nation, Jesus teaches us to endure the assaults of the enemies of the Gospel upon us personally. He goes a step further and says that we should even pray for them, do good to them, and lend to them. (Luke 6:35)

The prayer that Jabez prayed in the Old Testament should be interpreted in light of the prayers and teachings of Jesus and the disciples in the New Testament. We find no place in the New Testament where any respectable person prayed "Oh, Lord, Bless Me, and while You're at it... Bless Me a lot!". In fact, the prayers of Christ and His disciples recorded in the New Testament always concerned the advancement of the Gospel and the blessing and well being of others.

"I exhort therefore, that, first of all, supplications, prayers, intercessions, and giving of thanks, be made for all men... For this is good and acceptable in the sight of God our Saviour; Who will have all men to be saved, and to come to the knowledge of the truth." (1 Timothy, 2:1, 2:3)

Mario on Wall Street

Mario prayed the prayer that Jabez prayed. Mario prayed the prayer every morning for thirty days just as the author of the book said.

In his log he began to list the changes in his life on a daily basis.

On the first day- nothing *"miraculous"*. On the second day- no lavishing of *"honor and delight"*. On the third day he got up preparing to dart off to work only to find that he had a flat tire. On day four he gets an emergency call from out of state… *"…grandma died in her sleep last night, the funeral will be in Seattle day after tomorrow"*.

After several days of bad tidings Mario began to wonder if there was really *"supernatural blessings, influence, and power"* associated with the praying of this little Old Testament prayer, as the author of the little book promised.

On day five Mario awakens to find that America has been attacked by terrorists and that the nation is being plunged into a grievous conflict.

As a stock broker working in New York City, Mario had taken Bruce Wilkinson's advice… *"…if Jabez had worked on Wall Street he might have prayed, 'Lord, increase the value of my investment portfolio'."* But after months of decline his portfolios are still down 50% for the year. Two days later his supervisor at work calls him at home to tell him that the company is suffering financially and he is being laid off.

It is a rude awakening.

Mario tried to sell his house, but found no buyers. Unable to maintain his debts he began to default on the many payments he had racked up during the "good times". He now works a temporary job with the I.R.S. reviewing corporate returns.

Having lost the family's $300,000 home in the suburbs of New York, Mario has moved his family to the country where they live in a modest three bedroom double-wide mobile home. His excitement during the *"Jabez revolution"* has turned to depression. What once seemed so sweet has now left a bitter taste in his mouth. No longer in church, and spiritually disoriented, Mario's family is drifting on a sea of despair. "It must all be a lie", Mario thinks to himself, "All of my hopes and dreams have been dashed to the ground".

Like the destruction left in the wake of the television evangelist scandals of the 1980's, the fallout from the Jabez fad may also prove devastating.

It's as if the name of a formerly obscure Old Testament figure were a prophetic pronouncement upon a future generation that would turn his prayer into a daily ritual... after all, *"Jabez means pain"*.

Before the attacks on the United States in September of 2001 I wrote the following concerning the book "The Prayer of Jabez", by Bruce Wilkinson:

"The real damage of the Jabez fad is yet to be realized. Many Christians who have felt 'finally this is it... now I can get my life back on track' will fail to see (positive) change in their personal income, job status, and (perceived) ministry opportunities, and have their hopes dashed".

Yet all across our nation, in the months preceding the attacks, the prayer that was being prayed far more often than any other was, *"Bless Me, Lord, Bless Me indeed"*. What happened? Many Christians were left saying, "If this is what it means to be blessed, then I don't want any of it".

The church in America had forgotten the "prize of the upward call of God in Christ Jesus". We were so *self-centered* in our prayer lives that we stopped praying for our nation, and our leaders. We stopped praying for national repentance and *revival*. We stopped praying for the poor and the *hungry*. And setting ourselves ahead of everything that is dear to the heart of God we prayed, *"Oh, Lord, I beg you, first and most... Bless **Me**"*.

Like the church of Laodicea in the book of the Revelation in the Bible we have been neither cold nor hot. We have not been cold to the things of the world. We have not been on fire for the things of God.

The Apostle John records the words of Christ spoken about this lukewarm, self-indulging church, **"So then because thou art neither cold nor hot, I will spew thee out of my mouth. Because thou sayest, I am rich, and increased in goods, and have need of nothing; and knowest not that thou art wretched, and miserable, and poor, and blind, and naked"**.

Jesus went on to counsel us to buy of Him "gold tried in the fire". This gold is not found in yellow bricks stored in the vaults of the U.S. treasury. It is a treasure in these earthly vessels that is purified by the fire of the trial of our faith in Christ Jesus our Lord.

The church in America is needed now more than ever. People are searching for answers, and we know the One who has all the answers! Many around us will be suffering in great need in the days and months and years to come. The fields are ripe unto the harvest. The wounds of our nation and the world are great, but we know the "Great Physician".

Let us go forth now, **"redeeming the time, for the days are short"**. We must sacrifice ourselves in the coming years, taking up our cross and following in the footsteps of Jesus. In repentance, in humility, **"binding up the broken-hearted"**, we preach "Christ and Him crucified", the only hope for mankind.

In our weakness, He will show Himself strong as we tell a lost a dying world of the love of a Savior who feels our deepest woe, who cures our mortal wound, who died that we might live, and by whose stripes we are healed.

"Beloved, think it not strange concerning the fiery trial which is to try you, as though some strange thing happened unto you...

But rejoice, in as much as ye are partakers of Christ's sufferings; that when His glory shall be revealed, ye may be glad also with exceeding joy...

That the trial of your faith, being much more precious than of gold which perisheth, though it be tried of fire, might be found unto praise and honour and glory at the appearing of Jesus Christ...

In the world ye shall have tribulation: but be of good cheer, I (Jesus) have overcome the world."

(1 Peter 4:12-13, 1:7, John 16:33)

10
Blessed Are...

The sub-title of "*The Prayer of Jabez*", by Bruce Wilkinson, is entitled, "*Breaking through to the Blessed Life*". The 93 pages which follow claim to teach the reader of the book "*how the remarkable prayer of a little-known Bible-hero can release God's favor, power, and protection... how one daily prayer can help you leave the past behind and break through to the life you were meant to live.*"

But it was Jesus who taught us what it truly means to be blessed of God. His Words from "The Sermon on the Mount" speak more on the subject of true blessedness than any other passages of Scripture in the Bible.

It is my prayer that the Words of Christ which follow will find a place in your heart this very hour... that you might go forward from this day forth knowing what it really means to break through to the *Blessed Life*...

Blessed are the poor in spirit: for theirs is the kingdom of heaven.

Blessed are they that mourn: for they shall be comforted.

Blessed are the meek: for they shall inherit the earth.

Blessed are they which do hunger and thirst after righteousness: for they shall be filled.

Blessed are the merciful: for they shall obtain mercy.

Blessed are the pure in heart: for they shall see God.

Blessed are the peacemakers: for they shall be called the children of God.

Blessed are they which are persecuted for righteousness' sake: for their's is the kingdom of heaven.

Blessed are ye, when men shall revile you, and persecute you, and shall say all manner of evil against you falsely, for my sake.

Rejoice, and be exceeding glad: for great is your reward in heaven: for so persecuted they the prophets which were before you.

Ye are the salt of the earth: but if the salt have lost his savour, wherewith shall it be salted? It is thenceforth good for nothing, but to be cast out, and to be trodden under foot of men.

Ye are the light of the world. A city that is set on an hill cannot be hid.

Neither do men light a candle, and put it under a bushel, but on a candlestick; and it giveth light unto all that are in the house.

Let your light so shine before men, that they may see your good works, and glorify your Father which is in heaven.

References

(All references below are from the book 'The Prayer of Jabez' except
    for those noted as 'Jabez for Kids' or 'Jabez for Teens'.
    All three books were authored by Bruce H. Wilkinson.)

"Do you want to be extravagantly blessed by God? (Back cover)
...Pray the Jabez prayer every morning... (Pg. 86)
...only one sentence... tucked away in the Bible... (Preface, pg. 7)
...it contains the key to a life of extra-ordinary favor with God...
(Preface, pg. 7)
...I prayed the little prayer myself – word for word...(Pg. 4, Jabez
for Kids)
...I've been praying Jabez for more than half my life...(Pg. 16)
...The Jabez prayer distills God's powerful will for your
future...(Pg. 12)
...Follow unwaveringly the plan outlined here for the next thirty
days...(Pg. 86,)
...each of Jabez's requests can release something miraculous in
your life...(Pg. 15)
...release God's favor, power, and protection...(Back Cover)
...you can change your future...change what happens one minute
from now (Pg 29)
...you will change your legacy and bring supernatural blessings
wherever you go (Pg 91)
...supernatural blessing, influence, and power...(Pg. 62)
...little prayer... giant prize...(Pg. 9)
...bless me...and what I really mean is...bless me a lot!
(Pg.36, Jabez for Teens)
...nothing but God's fullest blessing will do...(Pg. 17)
...when you take little steps, you don't need God...(Pg. 44)
...thousands... are seeing miracles happen on a regular
basis...(Preface, Pg. 7)

...*your life will become marked by miracles...* (Pg. 24-25)
...*adventure, excitement, and lots of fun...* (Pg. 1, Jabez for Kids)
...*it's the kind of life He promises each of us...*
(Pg. 1, Jabez for Kids)
...*an exciting way to live - being partners with God...*
(Pg. 84, Jabez for Kids)
...*His only limitation is us-when we don't ask* (Pg 28 Jabez for Kids)
...*(be) not afraid to sound selfish...* (Pg. 19, Jabez for Kids)
...*(be) willing to ask God for whatever (you) want...*
(Pg. 19, Jabez for Kids)
...*you want something bigger... something huge...*
(Pg. 21, Jabez for Teens)
...*such a prayer is not the self-centered act it might appear*
(Pg. 19)
...*God wants you to be selfish in your prayers...* (Pg. 19)
...*to ask for more, and more again...* (Pg. 19)
...*much , much more than you've ever thought to ask Him for...* (Pg. 5, Jabez for Kids)
...*Lord, increase the value of my investment portfolios...* (Pg. 31)
...*you were redeemed for this: to ask Him for the God-sized best...* (Pg. 91)
...*we release God's power to accomplish His will...* (Pg. 48)
...*your want for God's plenty has been His will for your life from eternity past...* (Pg. 17)
...*seeking God's blessings is our ultimate act of worship...* (Pg. 49)
...*God will release His miraculous power in your life now. And for all eternity He will lavish on you His honor and delight"* (Pg. 92)

STEVE HOPKINS

The Hopkins Family

(A quick photo op at Burnet Bible Church!)

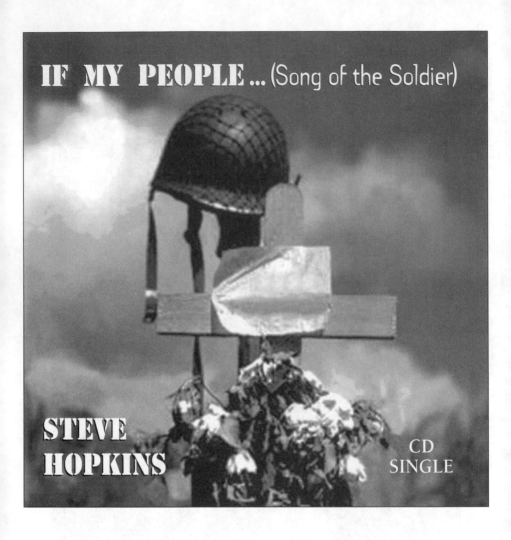

The new CD Single by Steve Hopkins, entitled
IF MY PEOPLE ... (Song of the Soldier)
is now available at fine stores everywhere!
or
order by mail, by sending $7.00 plus $1.50 S&H to:
If My People CD Single
Box 777 • Burnet, Texas 78611

IF MY PEOPLE...
(Song of the Soldier)

CD SINGLE
RUNNING TIME
4:13

PDW
Platinum
Discs
Worldwide
© 2001

COMPACT
disc
DIGITAL AUDIO

STEVE HOPKINS
www.platinumdiscsworldwide.com

Since the attacks on the United States more Americans have been waving the flag and going to church. But are Americans turning to God in repentance and humbling themselves? Steve Hopkins' song, "If My People," points us in that direction.

Jack Devault, Major (Ret.)
United States Air Force – WWII, Korea

There have been many songs written about the feelings of men who are about to go into combat...The ballad, "If My People," by Steve Hopkins, will bring a tear to the eye of many combat veterans... It brings back the memory of loneliness and hardship that our fighting men have been through in many battles throughout the world.

Eugene Z. Williams, Chief Warrant Officer (Ret.)
United States Army Special Forces – Vietnam

I think the young service men and women who are serving their country far from home will be moved by this song. I also think this song will help those without family in the service to understand the hardships of those who serve... and those they leave at home.

Wade M. Wheatley, Captain (former),
United States Marine Corp – Gulf War
USNA, Class of '85

IF MY PEOPLE ... (Song of the Soldier)

Mama, it's cold out here on the battlefield
And I've seen some things so terrible
   words just can't describe
Tell everyone I love them
And hug my brother and sister
And remember me when you say your
   prayers each night.

And Mama, please go and see that preacher
The one that spoke against the sins of
   America all the time
Tell him to speak boldly
Tell him to please keep praying
Cause we need to know that God is
   on our side
I can still remember the verse from the Bible
He quoted that Sunday night.

If My people
Which are called by My Name
Shall humble themselves
And seek My face
If they'll turn from their wicked ways
   and pray
I will forgive
And I'll hear from heaven
And heal their land

And she wrote back
Son, I got your letter early this morning
And these tears of joy words can't describe

Just knowing that you're alive
Everyone returns your love
And I hugged your brother and sister
And you know you're in our prayers
   both day and night

And I went just like you said to see
   that preacher
The one that spoke against the sins of
   America all the time
But his church said they had dismissed him
And the last anyone heard of him
He'd gone to be a chaplain on the
   front lines
And all he left was a letter behind.

And it read...

If My people
Which are called by My Name
Shall humble themselves
And seek My face
If they'll turn from their wicked ways
   and pray
I will forgive
And I'll hear from heaven
And heal their land

Oh, God's people
If we will humble ourselves
God will heal our land.

ALSO AVAILABLE

Steve Hopkins' dramatic message based on II Chronicles 7:14

For a free cassette copy
send your name, address, and zip code
along with
$2 for shipping and handling to:

II Chronicles 7:14
Free Cassette Offer
Box 777
Burnet, Texas 78611

(As always, if you are unable to afford any of
Steve Hopkins' ministry items, we will make them
available free of charge including S&H)